# 'Tell's Tales….My Best Stuff'

## Terry B. Wilkins OBE BA

'Tell's Tales....My Best Stuff.'

Published by Wilkins

Acknowledgements

Edited by John Yates & Simon Wilkins

Illustrations by Keith Wilkins

Cover design by Book Printing UK

Last proofreader, Methuselah (so blame him if any mistakes).

This book is dedicated to Mary, Steve, Simon, Chris and my late departed mother. I love them dearly.

# Introduction

A flight to the Antipodes from Heathrow takes about twenty-four hours. My wife Mary and I undertake this journey on average once every eighteen months to visit family in Australia and New Zealand. Listening to an mp3 player, watching films, reading, walking around, staring into blank space, talking to other passengers, sleeping, sighing, visiting the toilet, eating, drinking, repeating the process, represent the normal journey. I tried to be creative once, taking watercolours aboard to paint the odd picture or two, but with limited space, it was not easy.

In early 2010, on another sojourn, I decided to put pen to paper and write about things that have happened to and around me. My initial intent, to capture the amusing experiences, changed when I widened the scope to seek answers to family questions hitherto ignored. It has been an intriguing, challenging and rewarding experience.

I decided to self-publish, so in generations ahead the Wilkins family would be able to read of the adventures of a six-foot bald headed relative. But what does a person call a book intended for the family (and perhaps friends) without it appearing egotistical or stupid? Lying in bed, an idea emerged. Combine the more stimulating parts with an important aspect of my psyche...humour. 'A boring life? You must be joking.' It seemed catchy, not too pretentious. The working title?

The morning after the epiphany, I tested the idea on my two eldest sons, telling them nonchalantly that 'A boring life? You must be joking' would be the title of the book. Startled, they looked at each other in silence, mouths tightly pursing. Within seconds, they both exhaled emitting an embarrassed noise. Simon quietly started to repeat the title in a tone demonstrating disbelief.

"My father has written a book called..."

He stopped mid-sentence and unable to contain himself any longer, joined Steve in loud raucous laughter. Trying to make the best of a bad job, I joined in, before sarcastically encouraging them to suggest something better. I smiled inwardly when they asked for time to consider, feeling ground had been regained. Two days later, taking Simon to the airport for his return journey to Australia, I chided he had not made a single suggestion. After a short silence, he responded.

"I've got it. Why not call the book the phrase you continually use when you act silly but people do not find it funny. This is My Best Stuff?"

It had possibilities, so I adopted it as a working title. Steve later put forward an idea of his own, fortunately not associated with Dr Who or Gary Numan (a family joke).

"What about Tell's Tales?"

Such an astute play on words. Given the finished book would contain hopefully, memorable tales, it seemed possible to combine the two suggestions. 'Tell's Tales, My Best Stuff.' So there we have it, the splendid title courtesy of Steve and Simon.

# Contents

# Chapter 1
# 1943 - 1959

## Early Memories

During the Second World War, the Luftwaffe, in a two and a half year blitz, dropped 1852 tons of explosives on Birmingham. They concentrated on those factories producing vast quantities of arms, machinery and military supplies, hoping to destroy supply lines and shatter the morale of Birmingham's 400,000 civilian workforce. This resulted in the city being the most heavily bombed outside of London. Latch and Batchelor, an armament factory, under direct government control since the

 start of the conflict, became a constant target of enemy bombs, suffering several direct hits. My father, Raymond Barry Wilkins worked there as a forklift truck driver and lived just a mile away at 44, Berkeley Road, Hay Mills, with my mother Eileen and my brother Keith. I was born in the house, twenty-six months before the end of the war on 31 March 1943, weighing in at a massive 10lb 3oz. It must have been a desperately difficult time for my parents.

By the end of the war, 2241 Brummies had lost their lives, but somehow we survived unscathed, unlike the poor souls made homeless because of the 12,391 dwellings destroyed. It would be easy to blame the conflict, for my disruptive dysfunctional early childhood, but the reasons were far more complex. In those days, couples were expected to stay together no matter what the circumstances, the man dominating, the woman expected to know her place, singing to his tune. However, this did not happen with my parents. They separated shortly after

seeing me christened Terry Bertram Wilkins. The circumstances must have been harrowing. Keith, my older brother by four years, remained in the family home, whilst Mom took me with her when she left. Today, this occurrence would barely raise an eyebrow, but then a married woman on her own with child was uncommon and unacceptable.

Massive emotional decisions, without any possible reconciliation indicates it was a significant bust up with a lot of hurt and bitterness. Dad never talked about it. I did not probe. Occasionally Mom felt it necessary to be defensive.

"All my love went to the children."

"I want you to know I never deserted Keith."

"I was not having an affair."

Even today, I am not clear why it all happened. Many on my father's side are likely to know the true reason, but I never asked, preferring to accept the status quo, as it might have bought heartbreak, particularly for my mother. Invariably, very guarded on the subject, I surmised that she did not feel necessarily feel the innocent party. So why rock the boat.

When the acrimonious split happened, it put mother in an unenviable demanding position. With war still raging, Dad stopped his side of the family making any contact with her, destroying in an instant the hitherto excellent relationships she had enjoyed with his relatives. He clearly wanted total severance. By sending her 'to Coventry' he ensured she would feel the emotional pain of isolation and shame.

Mom now alone with child was in danger. John Bowlby, a post-war psychiatrist described the feelings existing at the time, "the neurotic character of the 'socially unacceptable' unmarried mother.' If so stigmatised, the potential existed for her to be condemned to an austere hostel, required to pray every day (twice on Sunday) for forgiveness of 'sins' after being marched to church, like a child. I cannot begin to imagine the stress. Ostracised, departing without Keith and potentially facing disgrace in the community, it must have broken the heart of a loving, gentle person passionate about family and friends.

## On her Own

Mom probably deflected any misconceptions by moving in with her sister, Rose Anderton and her family. They lived in Bolton Road, Small Heath, a prime area for German bombers, merely two miles from B.S.A. (Birmingham Small Arms Company) manufacturers of shell fuse wire, anti-submarine netting, aircraft and balloon cables. When researching I found a statement from a Ruby Langford, summarising the additional threat now faced.

*I lived in a back-to-back house in Bolton Road, Small Heath. At the back, a railway and the place where trains filled up with water. German planes*

*would follow the trains and bomb them. The homes at the back of us were bombed, but we were lucky.*

For eighteen months, Mom supported the war effort by working in a local factory on a pattern-making machine, before accepting a job as maid to a Doctor Hood. We moved into a large detached residence in Castle Bromwich, thirteen miles from Berkeley Road where his four-year-old pushy daughter and I would often play in the substantial grounds. Whilst visiting the country quarters in Swanage, her father discovered us sitting bare bottomed on a thunder box. He flew into a manic rage, blaming the young servant's son for leading his daughter astray!

We moved back with the Andertons after a year or so. The rear of the house backed into a communal yard, enclosed by a high brick wall where I frequently played with three cousins David, Barbara and Pat. We tolerated each other very well, apart from the occasion when, in a humdinger of a fight with David, I received a black eye. This is the first instance I can recall wanting to apply pain to someone.

## Ludlow Road, Alum Rock

When aged four, Jack came into my life. He was clearly Mom's boyfriend at the time we all moved into 65, Ludlow Road, Alum Rock, Birmingham 8. I do not remember meeting him before then. Mom assumed his surname to provide respectability. The title Mrs. Ridgers reduced the stigma of her 'living in sin.'

Peter Bridgwater lived at 81, Ludlow Road. From the instant, I said 'hello' as he walked past, we formed a close bond, the three-year age gap not hindering our friendship. We became best friends (and still are) spending hours together. We were opposites. My loud carefree approach contrasting with his thoughtful, inquisitive scientific mind. Peter loved experimenting but one test went horribly wrong in our living room. Interested in the construction of a golf ball, we sliced through the dimpled cover and elastic bands before pausing at the core. We could see white toothpaste like stuff, starting to push through a minute hole, when suddenly it exploded, the gooey middle shooting everywhere....over the tablecloth and worse, all over the wall. We tried to cover the marks, without success. Mom arrived, handling the matter with aplomb. She cleaned the mess as best she could, hoping to avoid Jack's anger (he had just decorated). Heavy marks remained on the wallpaper so as practical as ever, she hung a few pictures over the stains. On his return, Jack failed to notice the makeshift repairs. A narrow escape.

It took about ten minutes to walk to Anthony Road infant and junior school. The scholarly part passed me by, as I was more interested in girls, playing sport and fooling around. I fell in  love easily, displaying preferences on local walls by chalking who were the current belles. I would write 'Terry loves' followed by the initials of the fancied. The list, often six long, changed on a whim. Every morning the government provided all pupils with a small bottle of milk, followed at lunchtime by wholesome but tasteless canteen food. Consequently, the chip shop on the corner often benefited from children spending four pence of their weekly pocket money on fish and chips, rather than consuming the dreadful school meals.

Householders were more or less tolerant of children. Peter and I played polly on the mopstick, kick the can and cricket with many kids around our age in Ludlow Road or the adjoining Alderson Road. We also created our own games, a twenty-yard pavement football pitch with an entry at each end acting as the goal, the favourite. We respected our elders, rarely cheeky. Mind you, on a cold November 5 bonfire night, relationships could have changed, when one of our bangers, with a startlingly loud noise,   broke a bottle, a fragment hitting the front door of an old woman's abode.   A middle-aged man suddenly opened the front door angrily making a move toward us. Peter calmly and cannily sat on the pavement but with others I ran away as hard as I could, before hiding, frightened, behind a small wall. The man raged as he ran down the road searching for the miscreants. Luckily, he ran straight past me. Fortune smiled that night, as we all escaped his wrath.

Brandon Wade rarely joined our street games. His parents owned a grocery store and a tiny television. Every kid sought his favour hoping to peek at the new technology. I passed muster on a few occasions, marvelling at the black and white picture fed   magically into the living room. I knew we were too poor to own such a thing, so radio was the main source of our in-house entertainment, Dick Barton special agent every young man's hero.

I joined the Cub Scouts, attending the local hall every week to meet with like-minded kids. I wore a dark-green top with short khakis, playing team games interspersed with learning masculine things like sewing, cooking, tying knots. Once a year with other Cubs and Scouts, I would endure camping in a remote location out of love for Arcala. She had a special way of communicating with her eyes. I am still besotted.

Note in the group picture, a cub is not looking at the camera. Yes, it is yours truly, visually illustrating my inability, as a youth, to concentrate for more than a few seconds.

Notwithstanding, I became a 'sixer,' earning the right to stand out front and conduct the dyb dyb dyb, dob dob dob routine. When ten years old, after receiving the highest cub honour, a leaping wolf, I became a Boy Scout. Eager at the start, I left prematurely, disappointed that the new surroundings lacked stimulus but now able to howl with the best of them.

I remained blissfully ignorant of the hardship suffered after the war and although rationing continued until 1954, Mom managed the typical weekly personal allowance of a fresh egg, four-ounce of margarine and bacon, two-ounce of butter and tea, one-ounce of cheese without letting on how difficult it must have been. Occasionally she would use points pooled or saved to buy luxury items such as cereals, tinned goods, dried fruit, biscuits and jam. On the purchase of her personal indulgence, a tiny tin of salmon, she would exclaim triumphantly.

"I've got a treat today."

Grit and resilience shone through. It was rare to receive pocket money so I approached the local shop to be a paperboy. Some time later, earning ten shillings a week, morning and afternoon Monday to Saturday and once on a Sunday, I sorted and delivered local and national newspapers. On occasions, my cousin Pat would turn up unexpectedly. Her brother David, in later life revealed she thought we would marry one day!

Les, an imposing jovial smiling character, delivered milk and bread from a float pulled by his friendly steed, Dolly. They were a dream team. On command, Dolly would stop and remain in the same spot whilst Les attended to his customers, but when whistled would immediately trudge forward to where Les had now positioned himself...a remarkable display of tolerance, loyalty and obedience. Prolific in depositing waste on the road, the horse provided an opportunity for enterprising kids to earn a little pocket money. A local champion gardener never failed to offer a small reward for a bucket of the steaming mass. Slowly but surely though, horse drawn vehicles disappeared and by 1955, with road tax at £10 a year, three million automobiles confirmed the reality of the industrial revolution.

Jack, my mother's partner, often referred to me as 'son' in conversation and I called him 'dad.' That is how I saw him. A good man, with a strong ethic he never shirked his responsibilities. He worked for British Road Services, initially as a long-distance lorry driver, then as he aged, a clerk in the office. He won the News of the World prestigious 'Knight of the Road' recognition after a passing motorist saw him stop his lorry, get out of his cab and then help a disabled lady across the road. This typified his courteous nature. He carried a very heavy limp, suffering polio when young, but did not allow this disability to hinder activity. He played golf every week off a handicap of sixteen queuing at Pype Hayes, from as early as 6am on a Sunday to ensure a game with his friends.

Discipline at home was strict but fair, the importance of good manners and respect stressed continuously. As a ten-year-old, after back chatting Jack, he threatened to smack me. I brazenly boasted he would not dare, since only real fathers could hit children. I made a BIG mistake. He put me across his knee, before hitting my bare bottom repeatedly. I ran into the living room bawling loudly, refusing comfort from Mom. She eventually lost her patience.

"Anyone would think he had hit you!"

When told what had happened, she expressed surprise but backed his actions. It did the trick. I never challenged Jack again.

I tried very hard to please her and respected Jack for providing emotional support but I often found myself in the middle of their disagreements. This normally involved yelling, combined with occasional throwing of the odd article or three. Mom once wrote in the appropriate calendar space, "Sunday bloody Sunday" after one flare up.   He had strong views making it tough if she disagreed with him. However, on occasions, she would follow her instincts. He did not want a dog. Mother ignored him, smuggling a puppy back home hidden beneath a coat. Although initially furious, he soon calmed, Lassie becoming his dog. The same ritual existed with a budgerigar. Mom went out and acquired a cage, before collecting the blue bird from a neighbour's aviary. He again went mad, but soon 'Butch' had whistles only for him.

On 2 June 1953, the local community celebrated the Queen's Coronation. Having contributed into a fund for many months, residents of Ludlow and Alderson Road enjoyed a celebration far grander than adjoining streets. Long trestle tables in the middle of the road, bunting, Union Jacks everywhere, transformed the area, creating a wonderful uplifting emotional day, the community showing true party spirit. The Queen looking radiant represented the future, her charm and poise mesmerising as we watched on The Wade's tiny television.

## Visiting Father

I never saw my father until aged ten, when Mom allowed me to travel unaccompanied on public transport. Every Sunday at 11am in my best clothes, I would catch the 14 bus to Saltley, the 8 to Coventry Road, the 56 to Berkeley Road, Hay Mills, where an hour later, I would receive a warm welcome from Dad and his delightful resident housekeeper Olive. With Brother Keith and Stan (Olive's son), I would often play in the tiny picturesque garden with winding path, immaculate weed free manicured beds and fishpond. A small metal shelter protected Dad's workshop, where with amazing dexterity he repaired shoes. He would hold loose tacks in his mouth, remove them rapidly and in one swift movement hammer them into a shoe held on a last. With a Stanley knife, he then expertly shaped the leather. Although highly skilled at this craft, he saw it merely as a way to make ends meet. His full time job was as a forklift truck driver at Latch and Batchelor, where he remained all his working life.

I never questioned why Dad would happily pack me off after lunch, to watch black-and-white films at the local cinema, when I only visited on the Sabbath. It involved retracing the journey on the 56 bus to the Kingston Cinema in Small Heath where the audience would cheer Roy Rogers and Trigger, booing the bad folk, like a pantomime. I started to take an interest in the girls of a similar age, sitting in the sparse audience. Therefore, as you do, I would try to sit as adjacent as I dare, without being too obvious! This would be directly behind or a seat away in the same row. Slowly, I would manoeuvre within touching distance and if sensing a positive vibe, move casually into the seat next to the girl without saying a word. If brave enough, I would suddenly reach out to put an arm around the girl and freeze. Occasionally, I would finish with egg on my face, but surprisingly it often opened up friendly chat. I would return to Hay Mills on the 56, have tea with Dad before leaving at 6pm to catch the 56, 8, 14 bus back to Ludlow Road. The Sunday routine continued for several years and although enjoyable, it seemed more like a duty on both our parts with little emotional attachment.

I obviously believed a cinema was a good place to meet the opposite sex because when thirteen years old, with a mate, we found ourselves sitting next to two girls...what a surprise. Soon, we indulged in a little cuddling (and in my case, triple tounging). Get the picture! Before leaving, we made a quick decision to invite them to a nearby café. Surprisingly, they agreed. Holding hands, we walked from the cinema, elation turning to nerves when we realised in the light of day, the girls were nowhere as attractive as we thought. They were considerably older than we were, heavy in makeup and weight.

The gruesome twosome would be appropriate wording. Not a nice thing to say I know, especially considering our looks, but seriously, they were ugly. The stilted conversation and furtive looks indicated mutual dissatisfaction. These were not matches made in heaven. I could not help thinking about all the stuff with my tongue! We escorted them to the bus stop (chivalrous or what) to watch as they departed. On the bus home we laughed hysterically, other passengers no doubt upset at our apparent lack of respect, little realising we had survived the ordeal, escaping intact. Life is too precious to risk life and limb.

## 'The Blues'

I became a fan of Birmingham City Football Team (The Blues) from an early age. On a Saturday home game, my pal Peter and I would excitedly walk the thirty minutes to St. Andrews, pay the six pence entrance fee and position ourselves normally in the Tilton Road end, behind the goal. Things were not threatening, adults, children and visitors standing together, repartee rather than violence the order of the day. If not at full capacity, twenty minutes before the end of the game, officials would open the gates, allowing anyone to enter the ground free. We always felt safe, but sometimes in the confined exiting space we would occasionally be 'carried along' rather than have our feet on the ground. Thankfully, we never fell.

The Blues had a consistent reasonable team, normally playing in the top flight. The favourite player, a mercurial centre forward, Eddie Brown, involved fans in goal scoring celebrations. He would run into the crowd, giving high fives often shaking hands with the corner flag. Wikipedia describes him as 'a pioneer of the goal celebration.' I was particularly interested in watching goalkeepers, as this seemed to be my best position in the school team. Regarded as one of the best in England, Gil Merrick proved an excellent role model. He spent his entire career at Birmingham City playing more than seven-hundred games between 1939 and 1960. His consistency earned him twenty-three England caps. On the other hand, one of his successors, Jim Herriot, lasted only four years never really winning the fan's approval because of his weakness in catching high balls. However, author Alf Wight was less dismissive.

*Herriot is probably best known today for giving his name to the writer James Herriot, a Yorkshire vet whose real name was Alf Wight. Wight needed a pen name to comply with professional rules banning advertising and chose Jim Herriot's name after seeing him play exceptionally well for Birmingham City in a televised match against Manchester United. Jim Herriot is actually a trained bricklayer.*

*Source: Wikipedia*

At Wembley, I watched the Russian 'Black Panther' Lev Yashin considered by many, to be the best goalkeeper ever. As a member of a world eleven, he filled the goal with his 6'3" frame, able to catch the ball one handed. He barked instructions, constantly organising his defenders. Awesome. If pocket money allowed, Peter and I also tried to attend the F.A. Cup away games. Peter however, missed the quarterfinal in 1956 when The Blues met Sunderland F.C. at Roker Park. On this occasion, another friend Roderick Oates accompanied me. We had a great position behind the goal at the front. Thirteen years old, I kept cheekily chiding the video man to film us. I must have worn him down as he subsequently agreed, setting the scene.

"Imagine Eddie Brown has scored a goal. Go mad."

How could we turn down such an offer? We cheered, shouted, swung our rattles and hoped as the match started that the scenario would actually turn into a reality. I thought nothing

more about the matter. Later in the week, class chums said they had seen the piece on Pathe News at the local cinema. Needing an adult to accompany me, I asked Jack to take me but due to work commitments, he was unable to oblige until the following weekend.

On the big day, I sat through Humphrey Bogart in 'The Desperate Hours' waiting for the moment. With heart beating heavily, the news burst into action. Five minutes later, absolutely devastated, I listened, as the manager explained why the match did not feature. The newsreel automatically changed every seven days, on a Friday. We were twenty-four hours late.

Now, fast-forward fifty-four years. Peter and I are reminiscing about the match. We could not recall the date, so Googled the question. Astonishingly, the original newsreel of the game pops up. The footage shows an exuberant youngster at the front of the crowd, spinning his rattle for all its worth...quite surreal, very exciting! Examination of the still photos reveals the staging of the scene, as very few other fans are cheering. Peter recognised Roderick as my companion, due to the size of his ears.

Source: *www.britishpathe.com/record.php?id=40264*

The Blues reached their single Cup Final that year, losing 3-1 to Manchester City. Bert Trautmann, the German born Manchester City goalkeeper, famously completed the last seventeen minutes with a broken neck, having bravely dived at the feet of Peter Murphy. Unhappily, I did not see the game, failing to obtain tickets or watch Brandon's television.

## Off to Senior School

At eleven years of age, I moved to the all-boys senior school, Alston Road Secondary, a thirty-minute walk from home. The headmaster Mr. Pritchard established a strict regime. On the first day, form master Frankham, caned every pupil bar two

27

lucky ones, for talking, evidently wanting to welcome intakes to a disciplined corporal punishment environment! It was a humiliating painful experience and thankfully, more by luck than judgement, I managed to avoid the experience again.

The Wagger Warren Gang controlled the playground. Each member manufactured a small gap in the centre of their teeth so they could spit at their victim when bullying. Unable to perform the feat, not wanting to suffer their wrath, I created a neat minute hole by pushing a pin repeatedly through my two front teeth. This earned their grudging respect so they left me alone even though I did not join their clique and merely practiced spitting at the ground. Decay of two-front molars soon followed the consequences remaining for the rest of my life.

My early treatment at the hands of a local dentist (situated by The Pelham) proved very painful. Although apparently having gum-numbing injections, I felt a viciously sharp pain with every turn of the drill. Signalling for him to stop made no difference. Today dentists try to save teeth, but back then, even a tiny cavity resulted in the drilling and filling of the whole tooth. Over a twelve-month period, all my back double molars suffered this fate. Today practitioners categorise those dentists as 'butchers'. They were so cold, so calculated. For the past twenty years, Roger Edelman has treated my dental complications with skill and sympathy. He recently developed a complicated nine tooth front bridge to fill the chasm left by repeated extractions. He has a great sense of fun and like me, is a big fan of Derren Brown. Recently, we talked about our experiences when young, in particular, my peripheral involvement with the Wagger Warren Gang. We mused what would have happened if I had become actively associated with them. Life would certainly have been different that is for sure. Roger proffered the notion of the butterfly effect.

*The butterfly effect is a metaphor that encapsulates the concept of sensitive dependence on initial conditions in chaos theory; namely that small differences in the initial condition of a dynamical system may produce large variations in the long-term behaviour of the system. Although this may appear to be an esoteric and unusual behaviour, it is exhibited by very simple systems: for example, a ball placed at the crest of a hill might roll into any of several valleys depending on slight differences in initial position. The butterfly effect is a common trope in fiction when presenting scenarios involving time travel and with "what if" cases where one storyline diverges at the moment of a seemingly minor event resulting in two significantly different outcomes. Source: Wikipedia*

Term reports perpetually stated an inability to apply myself, average exam results reflecting this. I found it impossible to identify with the teachers except Mr. John Williams, an ex-army officer. He had a temper, often propelling the blackboard rubber at any student talking or annoying him. He would also on occasions chew chalk, leaving small white marks on his lips making him appear quite mad, but he struck a chord. I respected the order he bought to the class and his ability to raise the level of debate. At a parent's evening, aged thirteen, he said I had a decision to make. Drift through life or stop swanning around and make something of my life...he had no doubt heard I aspired to be a dustman. That evening Mr Williams touched a nerve. From then on, I tried harder, concentrated and started to behave.

At fifteen, following selection by the Birmingham Education Department, I carried the baton for the British Empire Games,  as it moved from Vancouver the venue in 1954, to Cardiff, Wales, for the 1958 event. Unlike the transferring of the Olympic torch, this ceremony consisted of passing a single baton from the old to new location. A photograph in the local paper showed a proud young man.

If I excelled any sport, it was at football. Excelled is the wrong word really, as it implies superior talent, a skill I could hardly claim. I did however represent the school, the league and Brookhill Boys, a Wolverhampton Wanderers nursery side in goal. Bill, the manager, attracted many 'stars' from the locality, fielding three teams of different ages, continually winning all honours available. For a time I thought, I might make it as a professional. Although scouts from Wolves watched, my performances never warranted an approach.   Bill often invited Phil Kelly, an Eire international, to join our training sessions. On two occasions when injured, Phil took our team to his home ground at Molineux. In one such match, held under floodlights (a revelation in those days) against foreign competition, I could hear from our position in the player's enclosure, the frantic voice of a mad man. Located in a private box above our enclosure, a sweating baldhead repeatedly hit the glass, his behaviour intimidating. A white coat would have been appropriate. Phil, trying to put our minds at rest advised that Stan Cullis the Wolverhampton Wanderers manager occupied the space! Apparently notorious for swearing, anger and throwing things, his banishment to the box, represented a pragmatic solution to the problem.

Peter and I would regularly go to a local swimming pool, fooling around the major objective. Periodically, we would visit Woodcock Street baths to 'enjoy' the full-length pool with an Olympic height diving structure. We unfailingly set out to jump off the five-metre high board into nine feet depth water, but each time chickened out at the last minute. However, on one momentous day, things changed. We stood on the board viewing the tiny space between marauding minute swimmers, doubting it could accept a dropping body. We had been here before, in the end invariably preferring the ignominy of climbing back down the steps watched by the other actors. On this occasion however, we pledged to jump together and as the bell rang, without hesitation we leapt into the void. Peter hit the water with an arm out. I went in with legs apart...do not ask why, I have no idea. The water hit my private parts like a punch. I crawled out of the pool, bravely running into the dressing room, hurting like hell. Peter, no doubt stifling a laugh showed concern as I revealed the full extent of the injury...a swollen, bright red, right nut. The older wiser head provided reassurance all would be fine, except henceforth I would speak with a higher-pitched voice! Since then, I have occasionally been for the high jump but without such dire potential consequences.

## Outward-bound Trust

I applied for a Birmingham Education sponsorship to attend an outward-bound trust. The motivation must have been the challenge of the unknown because apart from occasional camping with the cubs and scouts I had rarely stayed away from home. After a series of tough interviews, I gained a place as one of three to represent the City. Having led a sheltered life, I followed the pre-course preparation avidly. Every evening, for six weeks beforehand, as per the joining instructions, I bathed my feet in vinegar to harden them off, surely a clue of things to come.

The day started at 6am. Every morning all attendees were required to stand naked in a communal shower, directly under an individual showerhead. When directed by the early rising instructor, we had to maintain downward pressure on a cord to activate the freezing icy cold water, pulled from Lake Ullswater. It cascaded down, triggering shock induced screams. Under normal circumstances, it would be natural to walk away, but such action here, without permission would have meant extra duties and much taunting...the word 'wimp' staying forever with the individual. The duration of the shower seemed like an eternity in the hands of the instructor. He would stand at the front fully clothed, hurriedly counting to eight seconds, before demonstrating his masochistic side by slowly shouting.

"Eight and a half...nine, no do *not* let go otherwise you will be in trouble...nine and a quarter...nine and a half...wait for it...ten."

Shower over, we then had to run around the perimeter of a snow-covered yard in shorts and pumps for fifteen minutes. Hating every minute, I kept wondering why I had applied. Supposed to be character building, it appeared to be a punishment rather than reward, though gradually on the establishment of routine, the stress levels lessened.

The days were about fitness, trekking, learning new skills around lakes or mountains, survival techniques, map reading, orienteering, team building. We left for our initial three day trek well trained, spending the opening night in a bivouac on a mountainside. In the morning, I awoke with a massive headache and a swollen right eye, forcing the instructors to accompany me back to base camp. After examination, confined to a mirrorless sick bay, I inhaled pungent vapours every hour for fifteen minutes and consumed pills to ease the pain. Two days later, with sirens blaring, an ambulance transferred me to Carlisle hospital, fifty miles away, where immediately on arrival a team of specialists started their examination. Whilst scary, assurances were given all would be well. They wrapped a heavy bandage around my head and over the eye to protect the swelling. A loving letter soon arrived from Mom expressing concern. She had received a phone call from my course tutor.

A doctor diagnosed the problem as a heavy sinus infection complicated by the growth of a carbuncle. This explained the removal of the mirrors from the sick bay. I looked out of place in the ward, most of the patients about the age I am now. Visitors to other patients were very sympathetic, often stopping for a chat, generously donating confectionary. The nurses were great. I guess having a young cheeky chap in their midst helped to lighten their burden of dealing with the 'aged.' A frail religious person with the title 'Canon' inhabited the bed, two away from mine. A nurse with a twinkle in her eye told me she did not appreciate his title, until viewing what he had between his legs!

After a ten-day stay, I re-joined teammates at base camp fully recovered and participated in all remaining activities. At the end, understanding instructors kindly presented me with the course badge. Notwithstanding the freezing cold showers, I absolutely loved the teamwork, self-discipline and relationship building. The experience taught everything good, discouraging everything bad...fantastic life training.

## Senior Prefect

Returning to school wiser, I settled in quickly determined to make the most of the experience. A year later, appointed head boy, I led a team of sixteen prefects. Blazer, grey slacks and black shoes were the order of the day...and a good mop of coiffured hair!

## Earning a Wage

I left school at 15years 9months, with an O-level (for English), six GCSEs, determined to follow a career as a police officer. I had decided what sort of person I wanted to be. Mr. Pritchard and Mr. Williams had helped me avoid heavy trouble. God knows what would have happened if they had not.

I knew by now I had the capability to make something of my life and upholding the law created such an opportunity. However, unable to apply for a cadet position for another nine months, I immediately started a salaried job, working in a traditional hardware shop located in Bordesley Green, near the school. I had often spoken to the owner, Mr. Howe, as he stood in his customary brown cow gown, in the doorway of his property. He knew of my career intentions but even so employed me as a shop assistant. Learning the hundreds of products seemed easy compared to recollecting their locations. Every nook contained bits and pieces covered with cobwebs. Mr Howe happily explained how it all worked, profit and loss becoming part of my vocabulary, his pricing philosophy simple.

"Double what I paid for it. Put that price on the label."

His trade model, to provide specialist goods rather than bulk meant margins had to be good, though to a young man making his way, the profit seemed excessive. Mr. Howe also employed a firefighter who moonlighted during his time off. Once a week we travelled to the Stoke area to collect earthenware from various potteries. The workers were forever bantering, their activity intense. A considerable sexual chemistry existed between the most unlikely people, a bit of this and that, often-taking place behind the stack of plates. After six months employment, I applied to join the cadets, Mr Howe generously allowing me to attend a series of interviews at Birmingham Police H.Q, Steelhouse Lane.

An increasing maturity, thank goodness, diminished somewhat my ability to do stupid things though not completely. Brian, a friend from secondary school contracted a muscle wasting disease, and by the age of sixteen, his limb movements were severely restricted. I spent many a day with Brian trying to help him through the ordeal, my lingering adolescence surfacing occasionally, egged on by his enthusiasm. We would form a racetrack around his living room, taking turns to 'drive' his wheelchair, with the aim to be fastest. Not surprisingly, we started to ruin the carpet, much to the annoyance of his adorable mother Lily. However, this mild bit of nonsense paled into insignificance compared to the day I accompanied Brian in his blue Reliant Robin three-wheel invalid car, designed for a single person. I curled up on the floor by his feet; head down. They were not long journeys, a mere five miles to the park. If caught, the consequences could have been dire, Brian would have lost his licence and the job I coveted would have been at risk. How utterly stupid, to endanger life, limb and the future. We should have known better. The invalid car stowaway made three appearances before we both realised the fun did not justify the risk. I wonder how my career would have turned out had an accident happened?

# Chapter 2
# 1960 - 1979

## Meeting my Future Wife

The number 14 bus ran regularly past the bottom of Ludlow Road on its way to and from Birmingham City Centre. The bus stop was not where Peter and I expected to meet our future wives but on one mid 1960 spring day, Marion and Mary joined the queue. They were stunningly attractive. Identical in every way, peas in a pod, long flowing dark hair, slim, wearing matching clothes, white blouse, red skirts. Smitten immediately, we both wanted to see more of them and several chance meetings later, it happened. The twins, sixteen, both fancied Peter (I did not know this at the time). Marion snagged the prize, her sister agreeing to tag along with the runner up purely as support.

I was really attracted to Mary but for three months, my future wife merely tolerated a tall gangly, unkempt boy. Hanging in there under protest, she remained distant, our relationship doomed to failure until in the front room of Peter's residence, to relieve the boredom of 'getting nowhere,' I offered to make a cup of tea. Mary will tell you in that instant she made a life changing decision, deciding her beau was 'not too bad.' Things improved greatly thereafter and we spent as much time together as possible. I did however, early on, take a break from courting Mary to cycle 100 miles to Rhyl with Peter (no idea why) intending to camp for a week. We both missed the girls dreadfully, so after three days we cut short the holiday to cycle all the way back.

We must have been madly in love or maybe scared they might find someone else if we were away too long! Certainly, I had a

jealous streak, which Mary rightly hated. Her father had exhibited this characteristic all his life so understandably she did not want to tolerate such behaviour. Occasionally I overreacted or misread situations. I did conquer the problem, though not instantly.

P.S. Interesting fact. Mary is always standing on the right of Marion in posed photographs. Eat your hearts out, Ant and Dec.

## The Police Cadets

Two months after the interview, at the age of sixteen-years-six-months, I left Mr. Howe to join Birmingham City Police as Cadet 90 Wilkins. A salaried position paying £4.89 a week, it shaped the rest of my life.

Whilst collecting my uniform I bumped into another new recruit, Cadet 83 Peter Fletcher and from that juncture, we became buddies. In an adjacent room we listened together as an officer outlined the impressive two-year curriculum, designed to ensure well-trained, mature individuals would have an excellent chance of making a success in a law enforcement career.

"You will work in a different department every quarter to ensure knowledge and understanding. You will receive an assessment of attainment at the end of each period and issues discussed. If problems persist, you will probably not survive. Once a week, you will attend pre-determined fitness and drill sessions to improve health and discipline. You will, at all times conduct yourself in a manner expected of a police officer. Failure to do this will result in instant dismissal."

My first assignment, The Midlands Criminal Record Office (MCRO) involved written recording of data, with little let up for conversation...a very sober location. In Head Office Admin, I delivered internal and external papers to the various departments many with exciting names such as the Criminal Investigation Department, Alien Department, Chief Constable's Office. Nobody said much but when a major crime had been committed, the atmosphere changed to electric.

The mounted branch was exactly the opposite, mucky and fun. The officers (jockeys) were a great bunch of fellows, their camaraderie superb. Practical jokers, they were not fussy about the status of their victims. On one such occasion, a jockey on hands and knees crept up behind a police motor cyclist who had stopped for a chat and painted white blanco up the seam of his polished black boots. Oblivious, the driver subsequently roared away on his 650cc motor bike with the graffiti marking clear for all to see. Although all hell let loose when the traffic officer discovered the wheeze, the jockeys simply carried on regardless, seemingly without a care in the world. Mary visited the stables once and we innocently left on our Ariel Leader motorbike without realising they had been up to their tricks again. On removal of my helmet, it became clear they had painted the inside with brown polish, the stain transferring to my forehead. Childish I know, but great fun.

The jockeys were deadly formal however when not playing. Four hours a day, they patrolled when not on ceremonial duty. On public display, their turnout and behaviour had to be immaculate. Six horses, standing between sixteen and eighteen hands, strutting their stuff guided by their specialist handler. In the stable, it was easy to see the strong loyalty bond between the two, as each handler also assumed responsibility for training, exercising and grooming their steed. At the start, my duties were restricted to ensuring the cleanliness of the stable. Mucking out, cleaning saddles, boots, stirrups and other kit. Eventually, after considerable on the job training, I reached a proficiency level able to groom without supervision. I could cope with all horses except one...Police Horse 246 Sultan (yes, they had numbers, like officers, as well as names). This stallion wanted his master, no one else. Of course, the experienced jockeys could handle everything Sultan could throw at them. As a novice, I steered clear of this monster. Nevertheless, I had no choice when, in the absence of his main jockey, the duty sergeant assigned me to groom him without supervision. I felt nervously proud as I started the task. Sultan, detecting apprehension, became restless, vigorously shaking his head, kicking out. Talking to him assuredly made no difference; he took control. I considered requesting assistance, but soldiered on, not wishing to lose credibility. Sultan resisted strongly as I tried to comb his mane but then seemed to calm a little and voluntarily lowered his head. For a second I regained control, or so I thought. Nuzzling up, head swaying, he nipped my tender parts with a perfect aim. I dropped down in pain, hugely embarrassed. Inspection revealed he had drawn blood and the need for treatment. The other jockeys openly laughed. I swear I heard Sultan 'neigh' in satisfaction.

After a tetanus injection, the insertion of a stitch in the wound, I returned to the stables to find Chief Inspector Goodwin, the boss, waiting.

"I have here a report prepared by a witness to the occurrence. It is titled Cadet 90 Wilkins has his tool bitten by Police Horse 246 Sultan."

Such lack of subtlety.

"The bulk of the report outlines the injury inflicted by the horse. I know he is tricky to handle but what I would like to know is how did it happen? Horses do not normally go round biting humans on the dick. Did you have it out?"

Of course, the jockeys were living up to their reputation as pranksters but the penny did not drop for some time given the collusion of the senior officer. Occasionally I have told this story at suitable dinner party and if brave enough have finished by saying, I still have the scar. Mary at this point would routinely remain quiet, no doubt hiding her embarrassment. That is, apart from the occasion, when she asked.

"Do you really have a scar?"

A searching provocative comment. Do I still have a scar? Not sure. I am now so old I cannot bend down enough to find out.

Two weeks before moving from the stables, I proposed to Chief Inspector Goodwin that cadets working in the stables should have the opportunity of riding a horse. Not in the normal curriculum, he appeared shocked at the suggestion. Nonetheless, seven days later, he called my bluff. Two inches of snow covered the freezing cold Edgbaston training ground as I mounted Police Horse 123 Diamond, the gentlest of them all. For an hour, the senior officer shouted instructions.

"Move the reins, tighten your leg muscles. Dig your heels in."

What started as a pleasant experience soon turned into pain as a raw posterior and crying leg tendons joined frozen hands in protesting. After an hour or so, Mr Goodwin called time, suggesting I canter to the far side of the field to join the others. My horse must have missed his mates because it suddenly bolted, taking me by surprise. Regaining balance, I immediately pulled sharply back on the reigns, yelling.

"Whoo, stop," or similar!

It made no difference, the horse continuing to gallop strongly. I had lost control. Frightened, I let go of the reins and grabbed Diamond around his neck remaining in that position until he joined his grazing friends. I had survived, more by luck than judgement. A 'sympathetic' jockey chuckled as he explained that pulling Diamond's head sharply to the side, not straight back would have stopped the charge. Hindsight is a wonderful thing. During the evening, Jack tenderly bathed the blisters, a reminder of a request too far. It would be another thirty years before I mounted a full-size horse again. Once bitten twice shy!

To reach the Coroner's office and deliver newspapers, involved passing deceased bodies. Often uncovered on slabs with identification labels hanging from their toes, the environment was not for the faint hearted. On occasions, air would expel unannounced from a body, inducing noise and slight movement. The first time I witnessed this bizarre occurrence, it scared me (as they say) half to death! I wondered why morticians, in their heavy green aprons, gloves and wellingtons, would want to do such a job. I hated the place, the pungent stale smell seemingly clinging to clothes even in the fresh air.

Occasionally cadets performed duties alongside regular officers. The best assignment, patrolling the touchline at St. Andrews, was a dream come true for a young football nut. You can sense from the photograph the stress I am feeling!

During one match, the referee, in the middle of a game, approached my mate Pete Fletcher as he stood on duty behind the goal posts.

"Someone is blowing a whistle in the crowd. It's putting the players off!"

Peter, a smart streetwise seventeen year old gave the best answer he could.

"I'll sort it out ref."

The game resumed and magically, the sound did not re-appear, indicating that reassurance and promising the impossible does occasionally work, especially if given by a young man bound for the top.

The regular exhaustive fitness regimes tested the limits of endurance. Weightlifting, gymnastics, bar work, strengthening exercises and basic self-defence featured strongly, combined with various competitive sports, such as volleyball and five a side football. The instructor Andy Baird, an ex-professional boxer who sparred with world champion Randy Turpin, not surprisingly also encouraged pugilism to toughen up raw recruits. Peter Fletcher and I were close, protective of each other, but we were also fiercely competitive. We had exchanged blows aggressively for thirty seconds when Andy stopped the carnage. He had no doubt concluded that rolling on the floor punching each other was against the Queensbury Rules. During a random session, I suffered a major mouth injury. Running around the gym, one of thirty trying to avoid capture, the forehead of another cadet hit me flush in the mouth. The dramatic impact uprooted two front teeth, the spitting hole disappearing in an instant. As blood gushed, Andy showed little sympathy. He said I should have been more alert! During the lengthy remedial treatment, I became the goalkeeper of choice for the cadet football team. In front of me, Pete Fletcher, a self-proclaimed 'they shall not pass' full back was a stopper in the true sense of the word. His intimidating presence and ankle length boots helped the cause, but in spite of what he might say, on the odd occasion the opposition did test my agility.

It was at this time, in 1960, that Mary and I were introduced to my father's new girl-friend Edie, a straight talking, no nonsense divorcee with three children. They had met at Butlin's holiday camp and spent much of their spare time together. It became obvious they had a special relationship as they openly showed their mutual affection and laughed a lot. On one occasion, Mary and I transported Edie to her home in Castle Bromwich witnessing Dad in courtship mode. It seemed a little surreal to see him kissing and cuddling in the back of the car. He seemed quite accomplished. Unlike his previous erstwhile romances, it did not finish after a year so it came as no surprise when she moved in with him, leaving Olive no choice but to move on.  At this time, having declined to give mother a divorce, Dad was still married.

### Duke of Edinburgh Award

 The potential to meet the Duke of Edinburgh at Buckingham Palace created the stimulus to undertake his scheme, so together with other cadets, including Pete Fletcher, I embraced the concept. My objective was simple. Achieve the gold level within two years, to coincide roughly with my move into the regulars. The official web site explains the endeavour better than I can.

*'A D of E programme is a real adventure from beginning to end. It does not matter who you are or where you are from. You just need to be aged between 14 and 24 and realise there's more to life than sitting on a sofa watching life pass you by. You can complete programmes at three levels, Bronze, Silver or Gold, which lead to a Duke of Edinburgh's Award. You achieve an award by completing a personal programme of activities in four sections (five if you're going for Gold).You'll find yourself helping people or the community, getting fitter, developing skills, going on an expedition and taking part in a residential activity (Gold only).*

*But here's the best bit - you get to choose what you do! Our programme can be full of activities and projects that get you buzzing. And along the way you'll pick up experiences, friends and talents that will stay with you for the rest of your life.' Source: Duke of Edinburgh Award website*

Having achieved the silver standard in nine months, I quickly attacked the top level. An obligatory section involved the need to follow a pursuit or hobby. Not really having a major interest, finding a suitable subject proved difficult. I have to assume, my 'O' level in English created the impetus to choose 'writing' from a pre-determined list! To obtain a qualifying mark, I had to compose a series of letters to a friend about a connected story, construct a creative poem and produce a biography of a well-known person. I selected the multi-talented G.K. Chesterton, an English writer, lay theologian, poet, philosopher, dramatist, journalist, orator, art critic and biographer. I have no idea why. The final section...writing a play, created the biggest challenge, so I visited a friend of a friend who masqueraded as an amateur playwright. Together we developed a ghostly masterpiece 'A Message from Nowhere.'

## Excerpt from script.

*Unexpectedly, technically impossible, a quiet faltering voice interrupts a radio programme.*

*"I am Brian. I died ten years ago in a boating accident. I am still alive but I know not where."*

*The radio programme resumes.*

*"Will someone please talk to me?"*

*The radio programme resumes.*

*"I am not stopping until I speak to someone."*

*Cut to the radio control room. The producer turns to one of his staff.*

*"What the hell is going on?*

Riveting stuff. Shakespeare would have been proud. I toiled through the other assignments eventually receiving a pass. No hidden talents emerged, so my 'hobby' finished as quickly as I had acquired it. Ironically, here I am fifty years later, again putting pen to paper and finding it just as difficult.

## Police Cadet Camp

Elan Valley in Powys, Wales, seventy square miles of lake and mountain countryside and six reservoirs is an area of outstanding beauty. The River Wye meanders its way through the territory.    Twenty miles from its source in the Cambrian Mountains, lies Rhyader.

 I had prepared well for my first one-month obligatory attendance at the Birmingham City Police owned campsite, three miles from this small market town, drawing on my Lake District experience. Based in an open field abutting the River Wye, the site consisted of a permanent kitchen/dining/recreational room, two large marquees (for the instructors) and six individual tents pitched in a row, each housing a team of ten cadets.

Activities involved everything to do with outdoor life. Conveniently, the camp qualified as the pursuit part of the Duke of Edinburgh's gold section, so if all went well a pass was achievable. Although more experienced than most cadets at this type of adventure, I did not relish all the activity, particularly the daily 7am keep fit, the one mile run uphill before breakfast, the trudging up mountains over uneven ground with a massive rucksack, cold, wet, suffering from feet blisters, sleeping in a bivouac on the side of mountain. Fortunately, the canoeing, cross-country running, assault course and sports activity made it bearable.  I had a simple survival strategy. Head down, ignore tiredness, hide any negative feelings from the more fervent participants, build on their energy, enjoy colleagues, and do not let them down. From the first day, instructors applied pressure. Lurching backwards abseiling down a sheer cliff face, relying on strangers to hold the rope firm and steady, soon tested the nerves. Team spirit grew rapidly and we quickly learned that by working together, seemingly impossible tasks were possible.

Mary and I certainly missed each other. Each evening we would put pen to paper, posting the correspondence daily. They were not single page letters either. Reams of nonsense really, except  the words plainly demonstrated how we felt about each other. The remote location deterred most visitors, but not Jack. He drove from Birmingham (a one hundred eighty mile return journey) bringing with him my mother, Marion, Peter and of course Mary who looked stunning.

The other cadets gazed in awe as the big black car, an Austin Princess, similar to a Rolls Royce, weaved its way down the single track to the camp. Only the very rich could afford such luxury in those days, so I have little doubt, Jack organised a deal with his employer, British Road Services (BRS). By having such a large car, he made sure I could spend a few hours with those who mattered. What a fantastic gesture.

To engender competitiveness, the Camp Commandant conducted a daily tent inspection looking to reward perfection. Inside he expected to see an immaculate uniform presentation with the knives, forks, spoons and billycans of each cadet, identically positioned on their ground sheet. Bad presentation or an item out of line would result in strong rebukes, poor team points. Outside, it was assumed the tent's domain (two yards wider than the fixing pegs and ten yards in front of the entrance) would be swept into lawn mower type lines and be free from every bit of loose grass, dust and sheep droppings. The intervention of nature made little difference; a bird deposit, a worm cast, a speck of anything on the grass at inspection, ruined any chance to gain the daily award of 'best kept tent'. On one occasion, the slow natural build up created worrying consequences for our group. With all the six teams lined up in silence outside their tent, two meandering sheep, started to feed on our neighbour's immaculate grass. Suddenly they turned, moving slowly in the direction of our neat tenderly prepared manicured ground. We held our breath. Providentially the sheep did not stray, walking instead, down the middle of our opponent's patch...dropping pooh as they went. In that instant, they were out of the day's game. We could not have engineered their demise any better if we had tried, so our smirks turned to sniggering. The Commandant saw our reaction. Annoyed, he dished out the severe punishment of kitchen jankers to our entire team. That evening for four hours, we cleaned the utensils and scrubbed the premises from top to bottom, whilst outside a loud inter-tent football match provided a constant reminder that laughing at other people's misfortune is not good practice. Perchance, this single incident, shaped my life-long aversion to the kitchen, you know, washing up, cooking, all that nonsense. Mary, are you buying this?

The small but symbolic flag would fly proudly outside of the front entrance of the triumphant tent for the next twenty-four hours. At the end of the month's course, the commandant would award an 'Overall Best Kept Tent' accolade. As you can imagine, what started as a chore and a giggle, after a very short period, assumed high-level importance.

Despite intense team rivalry, strong bonds formed between cadets as we all had much in common. Shorn as soon as we arrived, a silent siege mentality existed, all for one and one for all, them against us. The instructors (all police officers) kept their distance, never mixing. Disciplinarians, they found shouting at underperforming cadets normal. Imagine the way drill sergeants yell at soldiers and you get the picture. Strict rules applied...no alcohol, smoking, swearing or leaving camp without permission. Some local girls could not resist the temptation to visit a large umbrella tree on the perimeter of the camp, wooing the odd cadet here and there. These clandestine meetings were of no interest to me but I did have the odd ciggy and drink occasionally, despite the threat of expulsion.

The instructors, with ears to the ground, surely knew of such illegal activity, but sensibly turned a blind eye. During my last and third camp, I probably learned the reason why. I received an invitation to visit their tent - the inner sanctum – where cadets dared not go. After a little chitchat, I accepted an offer of a drink.

"Tea would be great."

"Wouldn't you like something stronger?"

I wondered what was happening as an instructor knelt on the ground and started peeling back a long rectangle piece of turf. Into view came an underground freezer, packed with beer.

Such double standards deserved a reaction but I calmly accepted their cordiality. Although feeling guilty I said nothing to tent colleagues, in an instant becoming part of the conspiracy, condoning the principle of 'them and us.' Why reveal everything? With no cadet expelled for drinking, why rock the boat. A quid pro quo perhaps? (Two years ago, I re-visited the now dormant site with Mary and a friend who lives in Wales. The umbrella tree still stood majestically. The field remained fallow. Sheep grazed, their droppings piling up on the ground we lovingly tended. I am sure a patch of fertile dark grass marked the location of the underground bar. Proof, if needed, that alcohol in moderation does no harm).

During the last weekend, participation in a ritualistic ceremony to engage with the local community was mandatory. Supposed to be fun, little enjoyment existed in an activity demeaning cadets whilst glorifying instructors. Via a twenty-yard long rope, fixed to both sides of a chariot type construction, sixty slaves (cadets) dressed in sack clothes, pulled the vehicle to Rhyader. Sitting pompously on top of the wagon, dressed in white wearing a crown, the commandant tried to look important. Walking alongside the chain gang, instructors dressed as Centurions, carrying whips, shouted their orders.

"Pull harder, stop slacking."

"Get a move on."

Locals turned out, cheering the train along the way. The instructors and the spectators enjoyed the procession. Many of the cadets did not!

Things changed for the better on the final night. Tradition allowed cadets to dish out a little grief of their own and throwing our tormentors into the freezing cold River Wye proved to be the most satisfying. Pete Fletcher though had his own ingenious idea. He shinned up the site's flagpole and replaced the Union Jack with the Camp Commandant's sparkling white underpants, borrowed after he sneaked into the private quarters of the head honcho. A cadet without fear.

## A Sad Reflection

Appropriately, Peter and I after two and a half years of courting, celebrated our engagement to the twins on the same day. Mary's three-diamond ring, purchased in the jewellery quarter of Birmingham, looked fantastic and I felt so proud that she had agreed to marry me. We were the best of friends, in love, things great. Then three months later, I attended a three-day residential course. The underground hub of scientists, police officers and administrators worked together to handle a simulated nuclear attack above ground. Cadets acted as runners. After ten hours of frantic activity, everyone met in the canteen, the evening point for relaxation. I sat next to an attractive girl called Dinah and conversation flowed. For some reason we agreed to see each other again after the course, leading to the following scenario.

'Boy meets girl while on a course. Boy becomes infatuated. Boy decides he needs to see girl again,  immediately breaks off his commitment to marry the girl he has been madly loved since they met.'

The words 'stupid' and 'naïve' come to mind.

Heartbroken, my ex-fiancée went on a spending spree and destroyed every photographic reminder of our relationship. She went to see my distraught Mom and Jack. They loved Mary and were very sympathetic. Jack predicted the fad would pass.

If I now continue with the story, you will see how apt those words are:

'Afterwards boy meets girl with whom he is infatuated on two occasions, soon realising he does not like her!'

 Stupid and naive or what?

Three weeks after the break up, I wrote to Mary, apologising profusely. I knew it would need a giant leap of faith to forgive a foolish young man.  I fretted about a future without her, but gradually she allowed me back into her life. We started to see each other secretly. Mary would accompany Marion and Peter and we would all meet up at a pre-arranged location. After destroying trust, Mary rightly needed reassurance that my emotions were genuine so we took it a step at a time. As confidence grew, we started to see each other more frequently and openly.

We resumed holding hands, the conversations more loving. I sensed her willingness to try again. After about four months, our renewed relationship had reached the stage where we would openly meet outside her parent's house in Foxton Road, Alum Rock. Crossing the threshold however, was a step too far, until one-day Gordon, Mary's eldest brother invited me in. Her parents, Lydia and Albert kept their distance at first, but once they realised we were a couple again, accepted me willingly back into the fold.

Normality and happiness returned. The trauma had made us stronger, wiser and more committed than ever. We became engaged again and vowed to spend the rest of our lives together.

Oh, I forget to mention. I broke off the engagement by letter. I did not even have the balls to tell Mary face to face. As I write now, I am still ashamed of the sorry episode.

## Initial Police Training

I left the cadets after two and a half years, having passed all exams with distinction - a marked improvement on my efforts at school! It had been a most enlightening, wonderful, life changing experience and working in ten departments had given me a most valuable insight into how the service functioned.

The following Monday, just after my nineteenth birthday, I joined the regulars, as a disciplined, mature, very ardent, Probationary Constable E 240 Wilkins. The three-month residential training course, at the Police College, Ryton-on-Dunsmore near Coventry, involved intensive study of the law and police powers. There were no guarantees. Failing the monthly examination, falling below the ethical standards or not reaching the overall standard meant a return to civvy street.

When not in the Nissen hut classroom, keeping fit and learning the practical side of policing took precedence. Stop and searching a suspect, handling an argumentative alcohol fuelled person, giving evidence in court, pulling a dummy from a pitch black smoke filled shed, saving a drowning person, learning self-defence...everything and more a beat copper may encounter. These short and sharp exercises involved few participants, but learning to direct traffic involved a theatrical production, a large amateur cast and inspiring music.

At first, we learnt hand signals by following the instructor. Then in group formation, we synchronised our movements to the dadadadada..da..da..da..da rhythm of The Blue Danube, blaring from portable speakers. A strange way to learn you might think, but the bizarre activity continued. You would think, the only way to learn is on the job with real cars, but at this training centre, the two-legged variety had to do. Standing in the four arms of an imaginary crossroad, student officers on command would silently move forward and when appropriate raise their arms to the left or right to indicate their manoeuvring intent. The fully uniformed trainee traffic officer, standing in the middle of the crossroad, had to react, regulate the surge and ensure safe passage for all concerned. Just like the real thing! Everyone dreaded the exercise, particularly the call to be the whirling-dervish pantomime dame in the centre, but false as it may seem, we quickly learned the pitfalls and the art. I did think of writing to the college at one stage to suggest that if the imaginary cars also mouthed engine noises it would be more realistic, but on reflection decided against it, as it would reduce the training to a farcical level!

The small imposing police sergeant responsible for this masterpiece also taught drill. With bulled boots, the peak of his flat cap pulled down in front of his eyes, he loudly barked orders, accompanied by a swagger stick. By a combination of verbal bullying, repetition, occasional reluctant plaudits, he soon knocked everyone into shape...except one young officer who marched left arm with left foot, right arm with right foot...'tick tocking'. He became fodder for the powerhouse of an instructor. Picked on unmercifully, he often sobbed in the billet, unable to see how he could correct the problem. Through his own determination and the expertise of fellow cadets, he eventually convinced his brain that marching was merely an aggressive form of walking and he became an important member of an impressive organised team.

When I look at our course photograph, several things stand out for me. How smart we all were. The lack of diversity amongst the twenty-two trainee officers. The fact the drill sergeant never went anywhere without his swagger stick. The latitude given to the PT instructor. The officer circled was the most handsome!

Early every Saturday, lovesick, trying not to speed, I would drive my Ariel Leader 250cc motorbike the thirty miles to Birmingham along the A45. Mind you, little opportunity existed for love, revision the order of the day. Mary, very patient, skilfully helped me learn verbatim the formal definitions, an essential part of the end of course examination.

At the end of the course, Rab Butler, Home Secretary conducted our passing out parade. The sergeant had done his job. With shoes bulled and well pressed uniforms sixty or so officers marched in unison, reacting as one to every command. Surprisingly, we even demonstrated the traffic signal drill to music with Rab looking on in bewilderment. You have probably guessed by now. I passed the course, finishing in the top quartile, progression into the regulars now a formality.

Whilst at Ryton, news arrived that I had achieved the necessary standard to pass the Duke of Edinburgh's gold standard. On 15 June 1962, during the last few days of the course, transported in an unmarked official car, I attended the award ceremony in the grounds of Buckingham Palace, where the Duke pinned the small imposing badge on my police uniform. It was a most wonderful uplifting proud occasion, enjoyed by few. Little did I know then that half a century later I would again receive an invitation to visit the palace, this time from the Queen.

P.S. Probationary Constable E 235 Fletcher also achieved the gold standard.

## On the Beat Training

I moved out of Ludlow Road, into Bordesley Green Police Station single men's quarters. Housing ten officers, the sparse accommodation contained one small communal area and a kitchen.

Small Heath nick, located approximately two miles away, became my duty station. Two hundred yards from St. Andrews football ground it faced directly onto the A45 Coventry Road. From the front, it appeared squashed between two retail shops. At the rear, a courtyard accommodated the occasional blue light vehicle. A functional old building, it offered no luxury, merely four cells, a charge room, three offices and a small canteen. The station catchment broke down into five beats. Areas 21/22 to the east, which included the house mother took me to when she and my father parted. Area 24, two miles of businesses and shops on the A45 Coventry Road and areas 35/36 the main railway conurbation to the west. On every shift, six beat officers, an inspector, a CID team of two, an office and foot sergeant covered the geographical area, plus in the day, several admin people. In essence, the same group of officers moved from shift to shift resulting in a strong team spirit. Most sergeants had been there, done that, but the inspectors were a breed apart. Rarely involved in scuffles or fights they seemed to see their job as picking up the pieces.

The working class area consisted of an eclectic mix of nationalities. Assaults were frequent, burglary and theft top of the non-violent list. Unemployment, lack of wealth stimulated a gang culture with clear evidence of racial discrimination and whilst this might sound a recipe for disaster, neighbourhoods tended to look after themselves.

During the first three months as a police officer, I doubled up with experienced officers to learn the ropes. We patrolled the streets, in a visible friendly manner keeping in touch with the community. We handled normal stuff like reporting motorists who broke the rules, locking up people who were drunk, arresting a few petty thieves. At this stage, the experienced officer made all tough decisions, so the practical training proved relatively stress free. I discovered where to obtain the best cup of tea, the areas the police had to be careful and occasionally exposed to the bizarre stuff not really falling within the realm of good practice.

"Have you seen life?" a training officer asked one night.

"Not really"

"Well you will tonight."

At 11.30pm, we trampled over rough ground, bulled boots in danger of damming contamination.

"Don't worry, they can be cleaned," he said.

At 11.45pm, we arrived at our destination. A playing field adjoining a narrow road.

"Lie down on this bit of raised ground."

"Why?"

"You'll see why in a minute or two."

He removed his helmet then casually lay down on his stomach to face a row of terraced dwellings. I felt wretched as I followed his lead. My unease soon changed to heart-beating anticipation when across the road, in an upstairs window, a radiant blonde in her mid-twenties, started to give an Oscar-winning performance as she removed her clothes. Excitement soon changed to dismay as I worried about the consequences if caught. The papers would have a field day, dismissal a certainty. My mentor though appeared very relaxed, as did two other officers who had also strategically positioned themselves out of sight, their police vehicle parked round the corner! With the exhibition apparently taking place twice a month, it was never a wasted journey. That night I experienced melodrama and regret all at once. We were acting like naughty children when we should have been making the streets safe. On returning to the station, the tell-tale sign of mud on boots and uniform were there for all to see. I worried the inspector, sir to me, would notice, so it came as a relief when on entering the building, I saw that he was brushing himself down. He too had been a peeping tom!

## Dinner with the Duke

On 24 October 1962, I attended a dinner with the Duke of Edinburgh, at the Lord Mayor's Parlour in Birmingham.

Twenty gold medal winners stood at the side of the splendidly adorned dinner table as His Royal Highness arrived. Following

God Save the Queen, the Duke made a short speech saying he looked forward to hearing about the experiences of his top award winners. An eerie silence followed, nineteen year olds finding conversation difficult with a man of such eminence. He cleverly broke the ice by recounting an amusing risqué story. Thereafter, conversation blossomed. Later that evening I asked if he swore to make everyone feel more at ease. He winked the answer.

## On my Own

The initial training with experienced officers, proved extremely beneficial. I now knew the fun elements of policing would act as a small but essential antidote to the difficult and emotional challenges that would arise. Having a strong mental capacity to deal with the mundane, the squalor, the outrageous, the dreadful, the stimulation and the unexpected would be essential. Walking the streets alone would test my mettle but I entered this new world with confidence, secure in the knowledge colleagues would, in a trice, drop everything to provide muscle if needed.

For the next twenty-one months of my probationary period, I learned the secrets necessary to be efficient at the job, trying at all times to prove I had the necessary attributes to be a substantive officer. Working eight hours a day, two week about shifts, with three days off during each fourteen days proved punishing at the start, but the walking and fresh air ensured a reasonable level of fitness. In reality the duty extended slightly beyond the eight hours as all officers were required to be in the station fifteen minutes before the official start of a new patrol, in order to receive the daily orders and show we were in possession of a truncheon, a Hudson whistle, a pocket book and pen, plus at night, a torch. Then come rain, hail, sleet or snow, we would walk the allocated beat.

Reassuring the law-abiding community whilst acting as a deterrent to those miscreants seeking gain by other people's misfortunes, provided my key motivation. I respectfully tipped my helmet to adults and bent down when talking to children, conveying hopefully a friendly accessible caring attitude.    If needs must, I could use a shift pedal cycle and assuming it could be prised away from the sergeants, a 'noddy bike'.

Barathea during the winter, thinner cotton for the summer comprised our functional clothing. A piece of kit stood out from any other...the cape. Warm, smart, distinguishable, its shape allowed for some informality. I could walk around, hands in pockets and no one knew. Throwing one side over a shoulder would leave an arm free to smoke (I was a ten-a-day man in those days).

If approached I would return the cape to its normal position to cover the lit cigarette, the public none the wiser...or so I thought. A teddy boy sussed it out.

"Are you smoking officer?"

"On your way son, don't be cheeky."

"You *are* smoking aren't you?"

"On your way son."

He ran away smiling, yelling as he did so.

"Smoke is coming up through your cape."

And it was...the shape of the neck acting as a funnel!

A colleague told his poncho story. After clearing a pub at the end of the night, the proprietor offered him a drink. In order to accept the offer, he manoeuvred the side of his cape over a shoulder. He started to consume the pint of beer, when he saw his inspector approaching. As quick as a flash he restored the cape to its normal shape, adeptly covering the drink in his hand...a similar strategy to the hiding of the cigarette. He thought 'sir' had been merely passing through but, on the contrary, he was required to accompany his boss to the address of a local criminal. With no time to ditch the beer, it sloshed around the glass and over his uniform as they walked down the road. Finding the abode empty, they both returned immediately to the pub. The inspector started to leave but clearly aware of his officer's deception, turned.

"Don't forget to return the glass to the bar!"

Priceless. The officer's uniform would have been even worse if he had combined his pint with fish and chips, so often the staple diet of a bobby. The cubbyhole cape also acted as an ideal hiding place for a battery alarm clock (a contingency in case a little nap was needed, but not the wind up type, they were too loud) a flask of coffee, anything really. So there you have it, all the tricks of the trade.

After four months on my own, following a call that an old man was missing, I broke a window in his house, gaining entry. A strange stale smell purveyed the air (like the mortuary) as I approached the man, lying in his bed, not moving. He felt cold, taut grey in appearance. Logic said he was deceased but feeling a faint pulse in his wrist, I telephoned the local on-duty doctor, who arrived fifteen minutes later. He immediately issued a death certificate.

"But I thought I felt a pulse."

"Tell me what you did officer."

Embarrassed I told the doctor, who smiled.

"What is the temperature of the body? What colour is it?"

"Cold and ashen."

He lifted the dead man's stiff-arm and let it go. It more or less stayed put. Rigor mortis had set in. He finally lessened stress levels by explaining I had probably felt my own pulse when feeling the old man's taut wrist. Police training whilst very detailed, tended to deal with operational issues rather than sudden death. Perhaps sensibly, they assumed a level of common sense, not demonstrated with my first dead body, would prevail. I learned a valuable life lesson that day. Never jump to quick conclusions. Work logically through a sensible process before making a decision.

We enjoyed one forty-five-minute refreshment break per eight-hour duty. During the day, jolly women employed from the locality typically provided a fry up, but on the night shift things changed.  From 12 midnight until 3am, an officer pulled off the beat, prepared and heated food left by afternoon canteen staff in time for the arrival of the troops, eager to enjoy their respite. My first and only attempt did not finish gloriously. The prepared pie went in the oven sixty minutes before the lads were due, the chips and peas into hot fat and water fifty minutes later. It seemed a good plan. When the first hungry officers arrived, I took the light golden coloured pie out of the oven, cut it into six pieces noticing in doing so, a creamy gooey pastry stuck to the knife. Unfazed, I proudly served the meals, expecting compliments to follow but the uncooked pastry and hard peas guaranteed understandable insults. Even though the chips went down well, a ban from the kitchen followed. Whilst having its compensations, it also meant I would never have the benefit of spending three hours in the dry on a cold or rainy night!

I did not take the job home, able to push any traumatic incidents to the back of my mind so life would remain as normal as possible. Mary and I made a conscious decision, unlike many of my colleagues, to maintain a social life outside the constabulary culture. I had witnessed officers seduced by the power authority can bring. I was determined to remain grounded and keep my feet firmly on the ground.

In April 1964, after serving the obligatory two years as a probationer, I received confirmation of my appointment as a fully-fledged copper, Police Constable E 240 Wilkins. No longer a probationer, I enjoyed a rise of £50 a year.

## Marriage

Marion and Peter married on 21 March 1964, at St. John's Church, Alum Rock, Birmingham, bringing their nuptials forward, from the planned joint wedding to purchase a new house.

In preparing for our wedding, I worried that Dad, still legally married to Mom, might react badly to seeing her again, but he gave assurances there would be no scene. Jack understood the sensitive situation, promising to fade into the background, asking merely a small favour...to be part of a special family photograph taken without Dad. Interestingly, separated with no communication over a twenty year period, both parents were now scheduled to meet twice in quick succession, as brother Keith and Val were also due to marry.

My stag party, a joint affair with two other police officers, held in a local pub attracted over fifty colleagues, no doubt drawn by the subsidised drinks. At the end of the evening, music greeted the arrival of the tar and feather group. No stupid pranks for this group, oh no, merely the important game of embarrassing three grooms simultaneously.

Moreover, the humiliation continued.

"Now repeat after me… I Tony take you Mary to be my wife," the Priest demanded in a quiet but assertive voice.

In that instant, I knew I should have corrected him, but instead without flinching I instinctively followed his lead, repeating verbatim his words.    Mary, radiant as ever, just smiled…knowingly.

Nothing was said either as the marriage register correctly recorded that Terry Bertram `Wilkins and Mary Alebon married on 3 October 1964 in Alum Rock Church.

Afterwards, guests were generously sympathetic as I tried to laugh off the embarrassment, but how stupid! Now every reader will know. I suspect my friends will have a field day.

Here I am Terry aka 'Tony' Wilkins with my lovely wife, brother Keith best man, Marion maid of honour, bridesmaids Suzanne, Kathleen, Linda, Jayne and our parents.

The reception at the British Road Services ballroom in Castle Bromwich cost £200. We enjoyed a substantial reduction from the list price, benefitting from Jack's employee discount. Those unaware of the history would never have dreamed of the acrimony between my parents. They even danced together, gliding across the floor as if they had been doing it forever. Very weird really, a little surreal. Together again, acting quite normally, when in reality they hated each other. Mind you, Dad apparently asked a friend when seeing Mom again after so many years.

"Who is that woman?"

Guests, presumably having knowledge of my appearance at the Town Hall with the Birmingham school choir, suggested I sing to Mary. A rendition of 'The Blues,' theme song, Harry Lauder's 'Keep Right on to the End of the Road' received my full attention. How romantic!

For Jack the event must have been difficult. During one of the most significant events in the life of his partner, he had to morph into a ghost. I wonder what my father thought of the unsatisfactory scenario, having created the problem by refusing to grant mother a dissolution. If he felt guilty, he did not show it. To add to Jack's misery, the 'special photograph' failed to materialise.

We arrived at the Merton 'Honeymoon' Hotel, Jersey, in the midst of a hurricane. We did not venture out often, the appalling weather ensuring we fully enjoyed our status as a newly married couple.

On our return, we moved into a first floor, police owned rent free flat, its imposing small balcony overlooking Kathleen Road, Yardley. Adjoining the main A45 and only five miles from my duty station with easy access to the city centre, it was ideally situated. We were young, very much in love with a reliable income. Life could not have been better.

## Birmingham City Police Football Team

Formed in 1905, Birmingham and District AFA, with fifteen divisions, set the standard for amateur teams in the Midlands. Over the years the Birmingham City Police football team established an awesome winning 'turn the other cheek' reputation in spite of the aggressive nature of the other teams trying to 'rile' and 'get their own back' on the constabulary. I became a permanent member of the police side after saving a penalty during my debut game when a cadet.

Our squad consisted of seven ex-professionals, content on extending their playing careers whilst moving into a worthwhile occupation with a pension. Not surprisingly, we were an immensely successful team heading the top division continuously and winning the national police championship five years in succession. During the latter stages of this competition, we would join the Aston Villa squad two mornings a week at their training ground in Trinity Road, Aston. I preferred playing to improving fitness so thoroughly enjoyed the friendly games against their senior team. We inevitably gave them a run for their money but on most occasions, their extra skill and fitness decided the game. On one occasion, I tipped the heavy laced brown ball over the bar following a left footed thunderbolt from Harry Burrows, a four-hundred appearance veteran. In doing so, I permanently deformed my middle finger. His reputation for having the strongest shot in the paid ranks seemed to have merit!

In Tipton, I broke my tibia immediately above the ankle. The coach, Keith Norman, an ex-Aston Villa player, said I had been a little late coming out...so much for sympathy. After an operation, I left hospital, leg and thigh encased in plaster of Paris and joined my grandmother, now living with us, on the sofa. She had also broken her leg. We made a fine pair.

Seven days later, on crutches, I returned to light duty work as an admin assistant in the Assize Court. Although boring I did sit through several interesting cases. The most infamous being the trial of 'copycat killer' Michael Copeland who in Germany murdered three people and killed again in the UK, with the identical modus operandi.

The build-up of dead skin beneath the plaster produced an incessant itch. In an attempt to gain relief, I vigorously pushed a large knitting pin up and down between the leg and plaster. Remarkably, within seconds the itching stopped, an almost orgasmic feeling taking its place...though how such a thing can happen in a leg is beyond me! I felt great, the joy real. Sadly, seconds later a sharp pain replaced the pleasure. It hurt. I felt awful. The action of scratching away the wasted skin had created relief, but in doing so the new membrane beneath had fractured, leaving the leg raw. After four months in plaster and weeks of physiotherapy, I resumed normal duties and started playing football again.

Annual matches against Glasgow Constabulary stirred considerable passion, national pride at stake. Cathkin Park (Third Lanark's ground) staged the game in Scotland and Villa Park (Aston Villa's ground) the return event. During a home match, a long high ball, punted from about thirty-five yards slipped through my grasp into the net. Team colleagues, unimpressed by the excuse newly installed floodlights had caused temporary blindness, knew I had committed a stupid childish error by failing to get everything behind the ball.

P.C. TERRY WILKINS
OF THE ST. ANDREW'S DIVISION
MAY WELL HAVE SAVED
GLASGOW'S PENALTY HAD
HE WORN HIS HELMET!

Fortunately, we won 6-1 so they treated me gently. Thankfully, the local newspaper missed the event, unlike the following year when the local pink Sports Argus printed a cartoon, cleverly demonstrating my inability to save a straight penalty shot. I twice toured with the team to Germany to play the Queens Own Dragoon Guards, in front of large numbers of troops, happy to demonstrate their talents at dissing visiting law officers. Occasionally we would play against a top provincial German side. On one such occasion, five thousand local rowdy people turned up. They must have thought we were a professional side ('The Blues' maybe). We won 3-1 and for once, I played extremely well.

Throwing myself at a marauding forward came naturally, producing occasional spectacular saves, but this gung-ho style merely masked a lack of confidence and technique. For this reason, I never considered myself more than competent, god given skills sustaining performance, rather than anything else. Nevertheless, I was still considered good enough to play for the best police team in the land and represented the Birmingham and District AFA twenty times over a four-year period, so I guess, I must have been reasonable. The Black Country Bugle 2004 certainly thought so.

*Among amateurs, representing Birmingham and District Works AFA was regarded as almost equal to getting an FA cap for a professional. (History of the Birmingham and District Works)*

Of course, I still had a job to do. Working shifts created havoc with the playing schedule and sleep pattern, but the force allowed four hours off duty when training or playing so this provided reasonable compensation!

## Afternoon Duty 2pm until 10pm

My least favourite shift. Up in the morning, see Mary off to her secretarial job with 3M UK, wait until 1pm and arrive at station in time for daily orders. Home about 10.30pm (assuming no emergencies) talk to Mary; watch a little TV before retiring.

To provide reassurance to the community a beat officer had to ensure actions and presence reflected confidence. I tried to look the part, treat people with respect but be firm and decisive when the need arose. Whilst I regarded as non-negotiable the arrest of a person committing crime, I preferred to give a verbal caution for minor offences such as litter, illegal parking, reasoning it would create a good impression of the service and the offender would be unlikely to digress again. Whilst firmly believing in this philosophy, I had worked as a cadet, at the division's administrative HQ in Acocks Green, recording in a log, all offences reported by every officer in the region. A summary offence received the notation 'S', misdemeanour an 'M', felony an 'F'.

Knowing the system led to constant examination of personal conscience, I felt a strong pressure to issue a summons after a four-week moratorium. In consequence, when finding a car in a no parking zone I acted, but felt guilty knowing a caution would have been appropriate. Later I cycled five miles, went off territory to correct the mistake. Two weeks later, the chief inspector (having received a letter of gratitude from the driver) expressed pleasure at the compliments passed, then strongly criticised my indecision, citing the effect this could have in a more acute case.

Situated in Coventry Road, a mile from the station, a local bingo hall became a constant focus for criminals out to make a quick buck, the preferred method of entry via a skylight, normally in the middle of the night. Out of frustration, burglars would often trash the place due to lack of money kept on the premises. After much cajoling, the owners eventually invested in a technology that sent an automatic telephone call to our station, ten minutes before activation at the bingo hall. This allowed officers to dash discretely to the scene, position themselves out of sight, believing the intruder could be caught red handed emerging from the premises. This seamless operation, perfected over several years, had resulted in many arrests so it seemed strange when a uniformed duty inspector positioned himself at the front door in full sight. In line with normal procedure, other officers attending remained out of sight. The alarm suddenly exploded into action, prompting the inspector to raise his truncheon, no doubt in anticipation that an intruder would emerge via 'his' exit. No one surfaced. I accompanied the key holder, wearing an overcoat over his fetching pyjamas, inside the building. Not a happy camper he complained about the crap technology citing the number of recent false alarms. After inspecting the premises, he confirmed abnormal damage to a rear door, distinctly raising the possibility the building had been broken into. The two-pip officer taking no chances still patrolled outside, his truncheon at the ready. Hiding behind a bar in the main hall, a frightened young man refused to budge when discovered, having seen the officer at the front ready to pounce! It took many minutes of reassurance to convince him he would not come to any harm. The arrest for breaking and entering followed shortly afterward. The inspector's new nickname 'Weary Williams' remained throughout the rest of his career after he lost the respect of his troops. Would he be capable of leading in a crisis? We did not think so.

Satisfyingly, a much more practical copper replaced him a year later. This officer enjoyed a full head of white hair, his vanity guaranteeing he would often turn up with his mane much darker than his natural colour. Dye preening occurred rarely with alpha officers, so he attracted many jokes amongst the ranks. Unlike his predecessor, he was a good officer in a crisis, so his credibility remained high, in spite of once arriving at the station with hair a purple type of colour. Yes, purple. Definitely embarrassed he wore his official flat hat all day even in the station. He looked ridiculous. A copper with coloured hair, an inspector to boot! In fairness, he did not go sick, and within ten days, his hair had reverted to its normal colour. It would have been refreshing to laugh and banter with him but being 'sir' this was never likely.

Several reports of lewd acts committed in public places near Small Heath Park prompted action to catch the offenders. A colleague and I kept discrete observations on opposite sides of the road, civvies covering our uniform. My mate, watching from a shop doorway opposite a toilet well known as a meeting place of gay men looking for sex, endured the ignominy of a passing man grabbing his private parts. A swift punch to the perpetrators face soon followed. Arriving at the scene, I could see the pedestrian slumped, holding his bleeding eye. The embarrassed officer decided on a low-key solution. Obtain personal details of the man and then let him go. Record the matter at the station, in the minor occurrence book (MOB), a simple invaluable tool for recording incidents considered inconsequential or not worth taking forward. Sadly, all efforts to extract the man's personal details failed, my mate becoming increasingly agitated at the thought of having to reveal the 'touch up' circumstances to his colleagues. On entering the station, the sergeant sensing something was up, insisted on hearing an explanation of the event. By now, a few other officers had gathered. The watching alpha males, guffawed without sympathy, as the story unfolded. Police badinage can be brutal. The man eventually confirmed where he lived, revealing his wife did not know of his secret life, hence the reluctance. The incident soon radiated across the service, developing a life of its own. Sadly, the colleague, poor soul, had to live with the incident throughout the rest of his career.

During football matches at St. Andrews, the Coventry Road nick became the central hub for all briefings, the recording of incidents, theft and lost property. Arrested spectators would end up in the station's cells, officers coping with any residuals. With an average of forty thousand people attending a game, match day proved an exciting if demanding experience.

The Hawthorns and Villa Park also fell within the remit of Birmingham City Constabulary, providing a great opportunity for over-time duty. As a football fan, it provided the chance to earn extra money and the potential to watch a first division match. I craved one of two assignments...regulating traffic (ten minutes after the kick off, officers with this duty would return to the ground and watch the match until fifteen minutes before the end) or better still, patrolling the pitch perimeter during the match (thoroughly enjoyed as a cadet). The frustrating alternative, an assignment to a fixed point outside the ground, such as watching parked cars, meant crowd noise represented the maximum excitement.

For the 1965 FA Cup semi-final, Liverpool versus Chelsea at Villa Park, I received the dream posting, traffic duty immediately outside the ground. Twelve minutes after kick off, I joined other officers in the player's entrance excited at the prospect of seeing the majority of the game from an advantageous position. One of these teams would reach the Cup Final, the atmosphere created by sixty thousand fans electric. Behind the Holte End goal, thirty minutes into the match, the creation of 'space' and the swell of additional noise indicated a fight was in progress between rival spectators. Officers walking the touchline waited for instructions. The inspector remained impassive, until the 'void' expanded indicating an expansion in the brawl. He then turned to officers lounging about by the player's entrance.

"You, you, you, go up. Stop the fighting."

I ran with colleagues round the pitch perimeter, the crowd appearing to follow our every movement. The altercation had stopped by the time we arrived, marauding opposition fans suddenly becoming good friends, bruised hands, small facial cuts and bloodied noses of no consequence. To reduce additional aggravation, we removed helmets, adopting a watching brief. When everything seemed normal, with colleagues, I made my way down to the pitch. The inspector suddenly arrived, instructing we stay "amongst them." Returning to stand with rival fans, I started to enjoy the game again, the scouse repartee fantastic. After about ten minutes into the second half, all hell let loose as fans in red celebrated a Liverpool goal. In an instant, ripped from my hand, I saw my helmet somersault in the air, then land somewhere amongst another group of spectators. Life flashed before me. How would I explain what happened? What would the person in possession do? What would mates think? Stunned, I pushed through the crowd to the spot where I thought the headgear had landed. It had of course disappeared, everyone denying complicity.

"Not me gov. I saw nothing."

The biggest indignity followed, walking the pitch perimeter, in front of the massive crowd with a bare head. Spectators had a field day. The lost headgear never saw the light of day again.

Encounters with inebriated citizens needed careful handling. There were happy drunks but also those who could turn vicious in a second. Restraining the aggressive lone person was manageable, but potential invariably existed for a major rumble if several people were involved. Accordingly, an unwritten rule existed. Stand back, let the fight sort itself out. If it continues, await arrival of colleagues, and then if necessary go in. The relatively low-key response at the cup semi-final, defused a potentially explosive incident, whereas an overly aggressive approach may have resulted in an instant 'band of brothers, them against us' attitude. A fellow officer, suffered from this phenomenon when two fighting drunks suddenly became mates and turned on him. He lived thereafter with a metal plate in his arm after trying to protect his head from an iron bar. Incidents like this resulting in injury were rare, but arresting any drunk demanded watchfulness, instant behaviour change a constant threat.

After a night in the cells, arrested drunks would appear in court, apologise and inevitably be fined a nominal amount. A formula to handle the throughput quickly, did not stop a rotund, balding police sergeant (acting as a court usher) delivering a master class if a persistent inebriant appeared in front of the magistrate. At the end of the brief hearing, the magistrate would address him.

"Are there any previous convictions?"

The sergeant, playing to the audience, would glance at the magistrate as if surprised by the question, look down and with fantastic timing, demonstrably jab his finger at the paper work in front of him pretending to add up each individual offence committed by the accused. When finished he would look up to deliver his findings in a slow deliberate voice.

"This is the defendant's eighty-fifth drunk and disorderly appearance your honour," another pause, "the last occasion being yesterday!"

As the court burst into laughter, the officer would look ahead without cracking his face. Fantastic theatre.

I imagine the strategy for coping with drunk pedestrians has not changed over time, unlike the way the police now deal with drivers suspected of being under the influence of alcohol. Today, breath test technology plays a part in determining the outcome. In the sixties, this luxury did not exist. A person (in this case a male) believed to be driving under the influence of drink or drugs (official words) would be engaged in conversation. If slurring his words or smelling of alcohol, he would be required to leave the vehicle, the officer observing any problems experienced in exiting or standing. Two crucial defining tests remained. If the driver could not walk in a straight line or touch the end of his nose with his index finger there would be reasonable cause to arrest the driver on suspicion of driving under the influence. Such a basic process, but it worked. Subsequent blood tests normally confirmed the officer's instinct.

A householder, yelling hysterically rushed into Regents Park Road. It was 6.45pm on Friday 22 November 1963. The assassination of President Kennedy's had just been announced on the radio. I accompanied her inside to listen to the terrible news. After ten minutes or so, I returned to the street where distraught residents gathered, many openly weeping. The misery continued for the rest of the shift as everyone attempted to understand what had happened.

## Night Duty 10pm until 6am

My second favourite shift as after a morning sleep, the afternoon and early evening were free.

On each night shift, an older experienced colleague would 'rest' in a local bakery for up to two hours. I found his attitude abhorrent and so did his superiors. They sacked him. Nonetheless, seeking a little respite, I too had a local arrangement...with a local automotive dealer. In an effort to prevent the theft of cars  from the forecourt, I agreed to sit in one of his vehicles for an hour on a pre-determined shift once a week, to keep observations. In return, the owner always left a flask of coffee in the car. Keeping watch in the warm, enjoying a hot drink, proved beneficial to both parties. I never caught anyone, yet curiously, the incidents decreased.

A week after starting independent patrol, a young confident woman no doubt observing youthful looks, pristine uniform, bulled shoes, welcomed me to the area at 1am in the morning. Her sheer see-through blouse, short fetching skirt, complemented by heavy makeup quickly confirmed her profession as a woman of the night...in spite of her snotty nose. The offence 'importuning for immoral purposes' immediately came to mind. She anticipated the potential action.

"This is my patch. I live at xxx  Golden Hillock Road. You can visit whenever you wish. Just ask for Carol. Your mates do!"

My head started to whirl, focus difficult. Why would she proposition an officer on foot patrol? Why would she be so open? Why would she admit colleagues had been to see her? Why was she so sure I would not arrest her?  It crossed my mind she could be under-cover, given her use of copper type language. Learning from the debacle of the alive/dead body, I decided to find out more, before taking action.

During the refreshment break at the station, I spoke to the station sergeant.

"I thought you should know serge I am going to arrest Carol from Golden Hillock Road."

He barked sharply, "No you are not."

I immediately thought…he's been there.

Thankfully, less sinister strategic reasons emerged. Kerb crawlers seeking prostitutes in Birmingham were inclined to visit the Balsall Heath area, a well-known red light district. Focussing police activity into this geographical area facilitated a certain amount of control. If the Small Heath area also gained a reputation for offering similar delights it would stretch resources too far, so the decision had been made to allow Carol (and a few others) a certain amount of latitude. For those who are wondering, I never visited her Golden Hillock abode. Oh, I forgot to tell you, she also doubled as an informant!

Any domestic disturbance needed careful managing. Disputes between couples were usual but potentially dangerous, one side inviting the police to the dispute, the other indignant. A word out of place would often see the atmosphere change instantly. Similar to the fighting drunks, the proponents could suddenly become joined at the hip again and turn instantly. If this happened, an immediate exit was essential. At a notorious dwelling in Bolton Road, the husband frequently mentally abused his wife, who regularly called the station. On one occasion, responding to a call, I found the screen of their television smashed, the man freely admitting responsibility because he disagreed over the choice of a TV programme. He complained aggressively of harassment asserting rightly, he could do what he liked with his own possessions. I left hastily. Six days later, his wife rang again. This time he had thrown a record player and the new television out of the window. He had reduced his spouse to a quivering wreck whilst never physically assaulting her. I left after she kissed him in response to his order. An entry in the MOB concluded the matter, at least until the next time.

The Malt Shovel public house on the corner of Muntz Street and Coventry Road was a popular meeting place for all sections of the community. A certain amount of natural segregation spontaneously occurred inside, but after closing time, the potential for conflict was high, as punters from all religions and regions congregated on the pavement. Every Friday and Saturday evening at throwing out time, the role of the two assigned officers was to keep the different races apart. We mainly succeeded in this, although anticipating fights between members of same community proved far more challenging!

A massive fight broke out in Tennyson Road between inebriated rival gangs. Local officers rushed to the scene, reinforced by car and motor cycle crews. It took an age to bring the incident under control with over thirty participants arrested. When back at the station I learned that most members of the Wagger Warren Gang had been involved, still bullying and intimidating. I peered through the cell inspection hatch at these arrogant sad souls, so grateful I had escaped their influence. Charged with causing a riot, they spent the next year in prison.

In the absence of definite instructions, officers were given discretion to work their assigned beat as they saw fit, apart the obligatory attendance four times a shift, at specific police points or telephone boxes. This enabled base at the pre-arranged time, to ring the officer and vice versa. Personal visits from the station were rare, but at 5am one morning, in the designated phone box, my sergeant found yours truly in full uniform fast asleep. Unkindly, he decided the slumber should end. Not by whispering, not by a tap on the shoulder but by instilling a jab to my private parts with his truncheon...such a rude awakening. After a real telling off, my boss expressed a small level of sympathy, suggesting a slower walk...like Dixon of Dock Green...would avoid the tiredness.

Handling loss of life became routine. Adopting a non-emotional, singularly professional approach ensured I could cope. Perhaps the way in which I handled a particular incident will leave you

shaking your head given my ideals. The midpoint under a forty-five foot wide Coventry Road bridge was technically, the border between Small Heath and Digbeth police stations but in reality, officers regarded the ground under the viaduct as no man's land. At 3am on a cold dark December morning, I could see the silhouette of a man sitting on the pavement in the middle of the bridge, head down. I moved toward him.

"Hello. You cannot stay here it will soon be daybreak. "

No answer. I lightly prodded him. No answer or movement. I repeated the action with more vigour. He fell with a thud. The man was dead (this time I had no doubt). Thoughts of the paper work led to a pragmatic decision. I dragged the body from the centre of the bridge to the Digbeth side, before propping it up. I slowly walked the hundred yards to a telephone box in Watery Lane, then pretending to be a civilian, dialled 999 to advise the location of the 'injured' person. On returning to the scene fifteen minutes later, the body had miraculously found its way to my side of the bridge with two officers from Digbeth standing guard. The excellent checkmate meant I finally dealt with the man as if nothing had happened. Fortunately, dead bodies cannot talk.

Listening for the exceptional, watching for the unexpected, dealing with the homeless, helping colleagues with incidents, trying doors, consisted the normal stress free night-shift routine. For the first three hours, the area would be relatively noisy, but an eerie still silence would descend after 1am, as the neighbourhood finally went to sleep. Well almost. The rear of a Co-operative bank of shops presented a good break-in opportunity for thieves, given its secluded nature and lack of light. Because of this, every keen police officer on beat 24 would attempt to dissuade potential offenders by visiting this

Daily Mail, Thursday, January 27, 1994

'Ignore it, Wilkins – he's probably got an upset stomach.'

area at least four times during a shift in spite of the major psychological challenge. The problem was not inspecting the premises in the pitch black with just a small torch, was not the danger of meeting a criminal, but the knowledge that large outdoor fridges might suddenly, without notice, spring into life with a crescendo of noise capable of waking the dead. I never conquered the frightening nerve jangling experience, the ever-present hot flush a constant reminder of human fallibility.

The commotion did not worry officer Keith, a lumbering loveable rascal. He had another reason for going to the rear of the Co-operative shops. For rest and recreation he would sit on the same toilet each time, helmet on, trousers and pants round ankles. We would often play the odd trick on him...making strange sounds to see how he would react... blowing our whistles to see how long it would take him to get dressed. Imagine then, how surprised a thief must have been when he dropped over a wall, having broken into the adjoining butcher's shop, to see Keith sitting on the loo. The thief recounted the meeting.

"I was scared shitless. I froze like a rabbit in the headlights of a car."

Not wanting to miss an opportunity to do real police work, Keith, a portly officer, stood up and fell onto the unfortunate criminal. We kept quiet when Keith received a commendation for his excellent work. His report read, 'as a result of information received I kept observations at the back of the Co-op when I saw...etcetera...etcetera.' Incidentally, the thief also kept schtum, presumably hoping to get preferential treatment in the future! This little episode cost Keith a lot in drinks, so he changed his ways. Thereafter he sat on the toilet seat without dropping his kecks.

On several occasions, my duty involved accompanying a grade one driver on patrol in a super-charged police car. Such exhilarating experiences. One minute cruising sedately, the next responding to an emergency call with blue light flashing, siren wailing. Remaining in control in these situations is vital.

Outwardly, I demonstrated coolness, whilst in reality my heart rate and adrenalin intensified in line with increased speeds. On the other hand, under great pressure, the highly skilled drivers demonstrated utmost composure. The superior expertise of these drivers shone like a beacon. Acquiring their competency level would have been a significant achievement, but I decided  early on, the best chance to advance lay elsewhere. With such an expensive training investment, promotion out of the traffic group was very rare. Riding a bicycle and the Velocette in consequence remained the height of my expectation.

At about 5am every morning, van drivers delivering to local shops would often throw a newspaper to an officer on the beat. If quiet, passing the last forty-five minutes of the shift reading the breaking stories, while moving slowly in the direction of the station, provided welcome relaxation before booking off.

By 5.45am all beat officers would be within hailing distance of the station ready to clock off the instant the next shift appeared. This would normally occur about ten minutes before the official end of the shift, a perk tired foot soldiers certainly appreciated.

## Morning Duty 6am until 2pm

The favourite shift. Complete the duty, relax in the afternoon, play golf or such like; spend evening with Mary.

Rising early at 5am did not present a problem, but in the summer, suffering from hay fever, I would often stand at the back of a shop doorway, helmet pulled down, until my puffy sticky red eyes assumed a degree of normality. Not a pretty sight.

The police station provided an important community focal point. Front counter duty involved dealing with streams of people reporting crimes, seeking a verbal fight, complaining or needing advice. On four occasions an old woman, not quite with it, visited the station to complain of a noise in her loft. Each time, an entry in the MOB was deemed sufficient. On the fifth visit, a neighbour confirmed her story so I went to the dwelling. On lifting the loft door, human stench leaked from the void. I levered myself into the loft space, to discover rows of sleeping bags, stretching far to my right. I could see a man made, three-foot hole in the internal brickwork, allowing 'free movement' between neighbouring lofts. The pensioner had indeed heard sounds in her loft...human sounds. The 'landlord' lived three doors away. Each evening he charged illegal immigrants rent to scale his loft. I trust he found his free bed in HM Prison agreeable.

The saga of the Dale Farm 'travellers' in 2011, reminded me of the occasions we were required to evict gypsies (we did not call them travellers in those days) about once per year. As if by magic, thirty or so caravans would suddenly appear on a piece of waste ground adjoining Garrison Lane. Inevitably, crime and nuisance complaints from locals would increase. The council regarded the invasion as trespass but arresting the offenders would not achieve the ultimate goal of moving the vehicles on quickly. Asking them politely to leave did not work either so alternative strategies had to be employed. Four or five days after their arrival, discussions with gypsy leaders, would lead to agreement for an orderly decampment date. Predictably, nothing much would happen on the appointed day, so threatening to serve unexecuted warrants (such as non-payment of fine, driving without insurance, no tax, failing to report accidents) facilitated sensible negotiations. Many would leave at this point, their summons remaining on file (allowing implementation on a future occasion if necessary). Those remaining now faced the heavy artillery. Early morning, accompanied by officers and dogs, several land rovers would tow all remaining vehicles off site. Compromise over, any sort of obstruction would spark immediate arrests. Sadly, it appeared the guests would deliberately leave their disgusting mark on the land. The barren terrain would now resemble an open landfill site, filth and garbage everywhere. Unimaginable putrescence, an obnoxious smell conveying the lack of sanitary facilities whilst abandoned dogs, puppies and cats scavenged, accompanied by the local rat population. Council workers (surely on double time) would subsequently move in and clear the ground, ironically making it possible for the caravans to return.

In Bordesley Green, early morning, a distressed man dashed into the street shouting frantically. Following him hurriedly into his home, a crying woman holding a limp, very young child over her shoulder, begged for assistance. The baby, bluish in colour, hardly breathing, appeared near to death...a horrible sombre sight. I ran to the local telephone box, dialling 999 before alternating between comforting the distraught mother and waiting impatiently outside for the ambulance. Eventually, after what seemed like an eternity, the cavalry arrived, parents and listless baby rushed to the local infirmary. Exhausted, emotionally drained, I retired to a roadside bench, hoping all would be well. The parents subsequently wrote a letter to the Chief Constable's office acknowledging my involvement in the baby's survival.

Arriving at a suite of shops on 24 December, a man prepared to destroy the window of a TV shop window with a brick. The smelly John Doe, of no fixed abode with little cheer, did not run away when approached.  Convinced he had not really intended to steal anything I directed him to the local Salvation Army hostel. As he made to leave, I walked away.  Hearing a loud cracking sound, I turned round. A record player in hand he stood by the broken plate-glass window. He smiled as I arrested him, safe in the knowledge he had achieved his objective of spending Christmas time in a cell.

The day after, at 12noon in Bolton Road, a woman standing in her doorway requested help.

"When will I know if the turkey is done?"

She must have thought a police officer would know everything; little realising this twenty year old did not even know which end of a turkey to stuff. By happy chance, I had heard my mother say 'you need twenty minutes for every pound in weight' so I conveyed this impressive logic. Disappointingly, she never even offered a beverage, unlike many other residents who at this time of year would often offer a drink or three.

Being the festive season, such generosity needed a positive response!

Ensuring the safe passage of children across busy roads presented an ideal opportunity to create a bond of trust. Chatting, holding their hands as they waited to cross, broke down barriers and built confidence in the police. To see them waving goodbye with a smile, engendered a real sense of pride. During the festive season, I would often receive cards and one headed 'to my favourite policeman,' written in a young person's handwriting, stands out. Such gratifying recognition helped the ego, though it could have been a case of mistaken identity if judged by an incident whilst on duty in Arden Road, Adderley Park. Standing in the middle of the road junction with arms raised in the traditional manner to stop traffic, I surprisingly saw Mary amongst the crowd crossing the road. As she passed, I said good morning, receiving a smile in response. After finishing duty, I rang her at work, asking if she recognised the handsome copper. She said she remembered seeing an officer, but did not think he was good-looking! In typical fashion, when learning the truth, she calmly said.

"I did not really take any notice."

How unreasonable to expect Mary to recognise her husband. After all, my hands were in the air, a helmet obscured part of my face, work clothes created bulk and I was all of two yards away from her! Priceless.

## Stephen is Born

Mary left employment with 3M, three months ahead of Stephen's arrival at 6lb 9oz on 24 May 1966 at 6.30am in

Kathleen Road, Yardley. A request for Mary to have our first born in hospital, received short shrift from the Council.

"She is fit and has carried well."

"But I might be on duty, not be able to get away."

"The midwife will be there."

I happened to be off duty when Mary experienced her first contraction, just after midnight on the day of the birth. Her mother arrived three hours later, following an exciting trip in a police car. The knowledge gained from having six children immediately paid dividends as she identified with absolute certainty her daughter was 'bearing down.'

"If you do not call the midwife straight away, I will have to deliver the baby."

After a six-hour labour, with assistance from the midwife, Stephen was born. We were both ecstatic. I skipped to the local paper shop excitedly telling anyone who would listen. Cards with news of the wonderful event were despatched to everyone.

A problem remained. The placental expulsion remained on the floor in the bedroom! We had received no disposal instructions. I wrapped the mass in paper, taking it to the police station boiler room in the station, next to the flat. After stoking for an hour, the temperature rose sufficiently to ensure the afterbirth incinerated. Not a job I would like to do again.

We were novices at the game. Steve cried most of his first day. We had difficulty placating him. Twelve hours after the birth I contacted the maternity ward of the local infirmary, seeking advice. The sympathetic nurse (who did not appear to be laughing under her breath) felt we should give our newly born as much food as he could possibly take. This did the trick; the poor fellow had been hungry!

I slept in the spare room on the second night in order to be fit for the morning shift the following day. Privileges did not exist for new parents. We had to get on with it. Mary coped as if experienced. She devoted her energy to Steve, introducing a fixed routine whilst also ensuring I did not feel pushed out.

## Mom's Bombshell

During an unscheduled visit, Mom nervously revealed what I already knew, that she and Jack were not married. This preceded her exciting news that father had finally agreed to a divorce after a twenty-three year separation. I gave her a big hug of happiness before making a passing comment that she would now be free to marry Jack. After a pregnant pause, it shook me to the core when she tearfully announced she had fallen out of love and planned to leave him. My mind was swimming. It seemed an age before I felt sufficiently composed to express amazement that given her new found 'freedom' she would turn away from the man who had been part of her life for at least nineteen years. I left Mom in tears but immediately regretted making such statements. What right did I have to interfere with her life? She must have had very good reasons why she would be prepared to throw everything away.

The following day, I called in again, apologising profusely for my inconsiderate unwarranted comments. Both emotional, we hugged as she burst into tears. A few days later, she offered the explanation that the news from Dad had created confusion in her mind and of course, she would marry Jack. Whilst feeling great relief, I felt uneasy my undue influence might have affected the outcome.

Having now decided to marry Edie, Dad cited adultery as grounds for the annulment. This infuriated mother but she was in a box. Whilst vehemently denying the accusation, she took the pragmatic decision to accept his terms in return for freedom. It seemed Dad had controlled everything from start to finish, bowing out with a final sting in the tail. This might well have been the case. However, understanding the law during this period, provides a possible alternative perspective, on the sequence of events. Marriage was considered a stabilising force during and after the war. Inflexible 1937 legislation supported this notion, allowing only adultery, cruelty, and three years desertion as grounds for matrimonial disunion. Guidance councils were not available until early 1950 and even then, a couple pursuing the dissolution route attracted the label 'absolute failures.' This stigma remained until the Divorce Reform Act 1969, when relationship breakdown became a legally acceptable reason for a judicial separation. Therefore, it is conceivable that Dad did not choose a vengeful route; he merely got the job done. The sanctity of marriage has certainly changed over the years. In 2013, 41% of marriages in the UK finished in divorce, two hundred times higher than a century ago. I wonder what Winston Churchill would have made of that.

## Attached to CID

Four years after joining the police service and now qualified for promotion to sergeant (in doing so, receiving £30 for passing the examinations) I moved into the Criminal Investigation Department (CID). As a detective, I now received a plain-clothes allowance and worked daily split shifts, 9am to 1pm, 6pm to 11pm with the occasional eight hour day or night duty. A working class multi-cultural community, many pubs, rival gangs and two well-known criminal families often led to explosions of violence, hatred and crime. A small team of four detectives found it impossible to cope, the 11pm booking off, a dream rather than reality. An arrest would inevitably mean three hours' office work, so any incident after 9pm resulted in extra duty. A CID job is not for the faint hearted. Only officers with a strong bounce back mentality survived the anti-social hours, gruesome violations and dealing with an undesirable fraternity.

We occasionally spent investigative periods in pubs and clubs hoping to hear a snippet of rumour or factual data that could make a difference. The nature of the job often involved obtaining intelligence from 'undesirables' in order to achieve the main objective of locking up criminals. This might seem perverse to those not prepared to see the bigger picture, but for the greater good, is it best to forgive small sins if in doing so, it results in the capture of bigger fish? In the United States, plea-bargaining is a legitimate tool. Here such deals are less obvious. The consequence of trying to obtain information, involved the occasional imbibing of too much alcohol in the fight for justice!

Information often arrived when least expected. Whilst on duty in the CID office, I received a call from a man who said he had knowledge of a robbery. I agreed to meet him clandestinely twenty-four hours later, in a quiet road, by railway sidings - yes like the films. A car screeched to a halt. Over six feet tall with a cleft palate, rough and ready as they come, he swaggered in my direction, holding his right hand tightly over his private parts. I thought it was a show of arrogance until he slowly lifted his fingers to reveal his penis skin entangled in the zip of his jeans.

Needing treatment, he urged me to take him to hospital about five miles away. This created a real dilemma. Should I call an ambulance with the likely loss of important information, or win his confidence by agreeing to act as his nursemaid. After receiving a few quick answers to questions, convinced his intelligence valuable, I drove him to East Birmingham Hospital.

On arrival, I jumped the queue. This tough person, his dignity removed, revealed the full extent of his problem. He did not appear fearsome any more, his posture displaying helplessness. Even so, when told he needed an injection in his manhood he suddenly sat up loudly rejecting the treatment. The doctor started to explain its importance when suddenly, without saying a word, the man grabbed the zip and yanked it downward prompting the release he wanted but at the same time, tearing the flesh of his penis. His jeans fell away, blood gushing, as he stood semi-naked. Although in severe pain, he remained silent. I started to feel sorry for him. The nurses rushed forward with swabs. He needed stitches and a tetanus injection, yet this big tough hard man again said no, apparently having a pathological fear of needles. I subsequently drove him back to our original meeting place where he revealed the reason for his phone call.

He knew of an imminent robbery and sought revenge on the gang member who had made advances to his wife whilst he languished in prison. Convinced he was telling the truth, detailed operational planning resulted in the arrest of four criminals caught in the act. Three months later, my informant, having committed a dangerous non-related felony received a sentence of five years returning to a prison he knew well...Winston Green. In his last incarceration, he had occupied a cell next to Charlie Wilson, the great train robber, who escaped from this maximum-security building by scaling the perimeter wall, then dropping into a lorry. I had indeed been dealing with a hard man.

Council owned houses dominated the area. Residents generated supply of gas and electricity by feeding money into their wall mounted meters. The temptation to break the unique lock and steal back the deposited funds was too much for some. Energy board inspectors, calling to empty the tin would immediately detect the crime. An open and shut case! Most incidents were as simple as this unlike the time an official found the prescribed lock intact with not a single penny in the receptacle. The homeowner had cleverly welded pipes from his house to that of a neighbour thus bypassing his own meters. In consequence, his gas and electricity was free. His entrepreneurial, but illegal enterprise soon ended abruptly.

A man in the area had a history of upping the sexual stakes. As a teenager, he received a caution after exposing himself to pedestrians from his bedroom window. He then started to 'flash' from his pedal cycle at any passing female. Disastrously, this led to occurrences far more sinister. Getting braver in search of advanced thrills, he continued to up the stakes by committing a series of indecent assaults. Probation failed to stop his antics. Sitting in the office one evening with a colleague, I received a report that a man answering roughly his description had committed a bad sexual assault on a very young child. We felt justified in questioning him, based on his history and the location of the crime.  Subdued at the start, he gained confidence when he realised we had no concrete evidence. We were struggling. The woman who reported the incident said she would not be able to identify the offender. The child was too young to provide any evidence, yet instinctively we knew we were sitting opposite the guilty party. He began to smirk at every question, baiting his inquisitors with past exploits. My rising anger reached a crescendo when, arrogantly without any fear, he said.

"I did it and enjoyed it gov. But you have no proof."

Outraged, I leapt across the table anger uncontrollable, but before landing a blow, a more experienced colleague restrained me. I left the interview room feeling cheated. Unfortunately, in those days, recording of interviews did not exist. Although the man had verbally admitted the grave offence we knew in court, he would deny it and accuse the police of collusion.  Superiors decided we needed independent corroborative evidence to make any case stick. He walked away without charge, but fearing he would commit other sexual offences, we covertly followed him 24/7. For two weeks, nothing happened...but then he stole a car. We arrested him, bang to rights, whilst at the wheel for 'take and drive away.' Pleading guilty, he received a two-year jail sentence, the maximum allowed. I understand he had a rough time. It was as if the Judge and the prison fraternity knew he had committed a heinous crime. He did not come to our attention again. After such a traumatic incident, I received fantastic support from colleagues of all levels, comradeship acting as a comfort blanket. Images of such a hateful person soon faded.

Attending court often formed part of a detective's day. I found it arduous to remain calm if a defence lawyer continually implied the evidence was a 'tissue of lies.' Experienced detectives handled this stress admirably, accepting it as a shrug of the shoulders game. I tended to take it more personally. I often felt then and still do, that Judges should take more responsibility for making communities safer, by sensible application of their powers. Michael Argyle QC, the controversial Recorder of Birmingham, from 1966 to 1970 certainly felt his sentencing strategy should send a message and he practised what he preached. Shortly after his appointment, he discovered that local criminals were dismantling public telephone kiosks by breaking into the cash box. Via the press, he announced a custodial sentence waited any person guilty of such an offence. At a stroke, he effectively restored 100% of the service by imposing a three-year sentence on the first perpetrators to come before him. As a High Court Judge, he adopted a similar tactic toward football hooligans, with similar dramatic results. He was tough but fair. He often demonstrated his genuine desire to help deserving cases by working through lunchtime to find them employment. Never frightened to speak his mind, he eventually resigned following criticism of the way he summed up the so-called 'Oz' magazine 1971 trial, when three editors were charged with  obscenity and conspiring to debauch and corrupt the morals of young children.

## Why not?

In the charge room, Owen, a superb officer, looked up.

"Terry, we are forming a self-build housing group. Would you like to join?"

"Yes, why not."

My answer was instant, without thought. What the heck. I had nothing to lose. Another scare brained scheme, which would never come off. I had signed up for a few of those in the past.

A couple of months later, Owen broke the unexpected news. The Council had allocated building land. Reality set in. I had committed to be part of ten strong team aiming to build ten houses from scratch in our spare time.  Scary stuff.

## The Approach

During the early part of the CID secondment, an unexpected conversation in the season of goodwill changed my whole life.

Every Christmas, Mary's old boss at 3M, Norman Deakin a regional sales manager, held a party at his home in Aldridge, Staffordshire. We would arrive in our second hand Morris 1000, park amongst the pristine sales representative's cars, my scruffiness the antithesis of the immaculately dressed sales team.   At one gathering, Roy Bartley, a West Country rep

suggested I had the attributes to be a successful sales person. It had never crossed my mind to be anything other than a law officer (and for a short period a dustman), yet I felt flattered to think people saw other possibilities. Mary not surprisingly, opined that she felt it unlikely I could do the job. We had a baby boy, lived comfortably in a rent-free apartment and I enjoyed the kudos. Why would I even want to consider the possibility? Suede shoes, big cars, sharp clothes, large salary, maybe. It could be an opportunity to improve our standard of living so I agreed to explore the possibility. We had nothing to lose.

Seven days later, I met Norman for a 'chat'. I felt very relaxed, convinced he could say nothing to change the current situation. I did not anticipate his brilliance. He had decided, quite rightly, he could never prise me away by talking about the job itself so decided instead to concentrate on the benefits. Judging the occasion perfectly, he employed every selling technique available (although of course I did not realise it then). He produced sales brochures featuring five different makes of car, asking my preference for model and colour. He gilded the lily by mentioning that representatives received a garaging and food allowance.

"We pay you to eat."

Although the starting salary with 3M would be similar to the £25 a fortnight net police pay, the extras, a superb incentive and an excellent final salary pension made the potential offer tempting. I left intrigued at the possibilities.

There were many things to consider. Mary had already voiced similar concerns to mine. Six months in a hardware shop hardly qualified as having sales experience. A change of job would disrupt our secure lives and we would lose our rent-free police flat. Where would we live? Homeless, with a little nine-month-old child, not a good scenario. The self-build group had secured land but we had no idea when it would start or finish. We were both rightly concerned at the risk factors. Although convinced 3M would be an excellent employer and Norman a supportive boss, the uncertainty of moving from a profession I loved with good promotion prospects, to unknown territory, legislated for rejecting the approach.

Further discussions with Norman took place. Changing tactics, he now concentrated on convincing me I would be able to sell and adapt to a new life. Gently persuasive, he told amusing stories of selling Avery scales, his former job. I felt relaxed in his company and trusted his judgement. The overall deal offered by 3M started to concentrate my mind, as the potential to improve the quality of our life seemed real.

Mother and Jack, although surprised, kindly agreed we could live with them, if the move took place. Confirmation of the self-build start date completed the jigsaw so after much soul-searching, we finally reached the decision to accept the offer, removing the possibility of having to live with 'what if' for the rest of our lives.

At Norman's residence with some trepidation, I gave a faltering performance relaying the decision. I thought he would be delighted but showing merely subdued pleasure, he instantly revealed he could not confirm the job offer, until resolution of a major political issue. This was the first I had heard of a problem and having agonised for so long, uncertainty returned. Stunned, bewildered, emotionally drained and demoralised, I considered walking away from the opportunity, but something told me to hang in there. Regular conversations with Norman revealed the issue. An established salesman from another part of the Company had applied for the vacancy and his executive could not accept that an ex-career police officer with no selling experience would be a better option. The odds of Norman winning the argument were not good but he demonstrated consummate skill during this period to maintain my interest. Finally, after a three month wait, he rang to confirm my appointment as a tape sales representative in Staffordshire, subject to references and approval from his boss Malcolm, the general marketing manager (GMM) of the tapes division.

Finishing at six in the morning, after eight hours working as the night shift CID officer, I caught a train to London to attend a formal job interview. The sumptuous reception at 3M's head office in Wigmore Street, West End, London, seemed worlds apart from the cold waiting area of the Birmingham City Police headquarters. Malcolm's swish office, able to accommodate a large desk, a six-foot diameter table, four chairs and a settee, reflected his position. After relating the history of the company, he commented on how tired I looked. On learning the reason, he raised his substantial eyebrows indicating surprise. Thereafter we merely chatted. He often told the story after I joined.

"How could I turn down such a responsible dedicated person who worked eight hours during the night in Birmingham, before travelling to London for an early morning interview?"

I returned to uniform duty to serve the obligatory three months' notice. I found a pair of police trousers with a sharp crease in my wardrobe and wore them with pride on my first shift back on the beat. On arriving home, it became apparent I had been walking around with a very bad noticeable scorch mark at the bottom of the right leg. I bet the wags had a field day.

Doubts remained about the correctness of the decision, but in a strange way, Chief Constable Sir Derek Capper helped settle the nerves. He expressed disappointment that excellent career prospects and overall conditions had failed to thwart the alternative offer. Whilst unable to reconcile my decision, he generously offered a lifeline, confirming that my qualifications and service (providing I repaid the superannuation contributions) would stand if I returned to the force within a two-year period. This extraordinary unexpected proposition provided much needed comfort. His reasonable and positive approach had the effect of removing any lingering concerns I had about leaving; it meant I could return if things did not work out. The last weeks as a police officer were anti-climactic. I merely went through the motions, trying to avoid any incident that could involve a future court appearance.

A local pub hosted the leaving bash. Toward the end of the evening, due I am sure to a reveller spiking my drink, I suddenly felt sick, tottering to the loo before falling back into the arms of a colleague who had followed behind. Twice during the five-mile journey home, the police car doubling as a taxi, stopped so I could hang out of the back door and throw up. On arrival, colleagues propelled me into the bedroom, where I collapsed on the bed in a heap. Waking fully dressed in the morning, I listened through a massive hangover as Mary admitted feigning sleep, having little sympathy for such drunkenness.

Later, with a thumping headache, wearing dark glasses, I said goodbye to teammates at the constabulary sports ground in Edgbaston, before returning issue clothing to the janitor. I retained just my own property...highly polished black boots.

I left employment with Birmingham City Police on 12 March 1967, after seven and a half years' service as a cadet and police officer, hoping that for a short period, in a little corner of the England, I made a difference. It was a life-changing experience. Working within the community, confronting dangerous people, dealing with maimed and dead bodies and handling any conceivable situation had given me a more rounded perspective. I now understood the importance of humour and the need to balance the good with the bad as a way of dealing with stress, real and imagined. Whilst somewhat apprehensive, I felt sure the experience would be a massive benefit in facing the future without the security of a uniform.

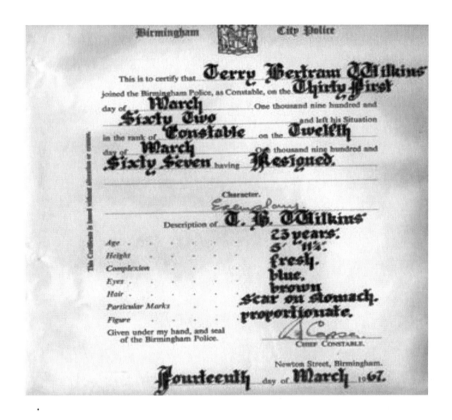

.

How things have changed. During my service, I extended to the community the courtesies expected from an old time copper, in return receiving respect most of the time. The public and the politicians expressed confidence in the police and consequently the press reported fairly. Whilst there were occasions when adrenalin pumped vigorously, I felt comfortable performing my duty and importantly Mary never worried. The job today has turned full somersault. Whereas, fifty years ago, a copper walked the beat alone with just a truncheon, whistle and torch, officers today have no choice but to wear body protection, carry mobile phones, panic alarms, eye spray, handcuffs and batons. They rarely act alone, are rarely on foot and allegedly spend 75% of their duty form filling, often driven by the need to cover their backs. The press expose any little mistake often apportioning blame without balanced reasoning. The trust relationship is under pressure. I doubt I could hack it in today's environment. I prefer to have memories of when a copper served the community on foot, in all weathers, day and night.

So what happened to PC E 235 Fletcher? Pete rose to the rank of Detective Superintendent. In addition to local duties, he spent several years in Uganda training their police in scenes of crime procedures and toward the end of his 31-year career, on secondment to the Home Office, helped develop with a scientist, the Electronic Facial Identification Technique (EFIT) the forerunner to the Identikit process. Not a bad C.V. for someone told during his first probationer appraisal that he was as smooth as a blocked drain!

## New Challenges

Mary and I were undergoing a seismic change. My stomach churned as we moved into Ludlow Road with Mom and Jack. The enormity of the decision weighed heavily. We had lost the rent-free flat, sacrificed job security and certain retirement after twenty-five years' service, to chase an opportunity. I tried to think only of the positives...if all went well, we would soon have a new house financed by a well-paid job with excellent prospects.

## The Self-Build Project

Destined to be one of the largest estates in Europe, with sixteen-thousand houses (including thirty-nine multi-storey blocks), the development of Chelmsley Wood followed the compulsory purchase of land by Birmingham City Council, seeking to answer the chronic housing shortage post war and the growth created by the industrial revolution. Emergency service personnel received a level of priority and several of the ten self-build groups were part of this strategy. The Council offer was simple and effective. They would loan money to the scheme on a staged basis, only expecting on a monthly basis repayment of the interest, during the building process. Upon completion, the capital outstanding, divided by the number of scheme members would determine each debt. Individual building society agreements would then see the council reimbursed. In our case this would result in our first ever mortgage.

Our thrown together self-build group comprised a police sergeant (secretary/self-taught electrician), five other police officers (ex-plumber, handy man, ex-apprentice electrician, two labourers), a builder (bricklayer), a building supervisor (foreman) and two others with no specific skills (my category). Our rules were simple. Everyone had to be on site twenty-four hours a week until completion. For me, this involved ten hours every Saturday and Sunday and four in the week. In addition to a full time occupation, this was a daunting commitment.

Our plot of land adjoined Sheepclose Drive at the north end of the estate. The scheme's objective, to build ten semi-detached dwellings drawn up by a local architect, allowed flexibility in fixture and fittings, within a standard framework. Such a brilliant concept relied upon a mixture of skilled, semi-skilled/partially trained and rank amateurs blending as a team.

Would it take three, four, five years or longer to finish. We did not know. We were entering the unknown.

The enormity of the task became apparent the instant I set foot on the unwelcoming, hard, barren ground with nine self-build colleagues. I knew the six police officers but three members were complete strangers. I introduced myself. They wanted to know my role in the group.

"I guess I will be a manual worker".

"You look as if you have never done physical work?"

My soft hands must have given them a clue!

As I stood there on 18 March 1967, I worried we had bitten off more than we could chew. There appeared to be too few genuinely skilled people. Forman Bill and bricklayer Alex were the two people with recent building experience, so under their expert supervision, during that first weekend, we marked out the ten individual plots. On the Monday, now dressed smartly, I started my new job with 3M. The challenge of commencing two new ventures within three days, knowing I would see very little of Mary and Steve, suddenly hit me. I needed constant reassurance, during the first week of our new life, that it would be all worthwhile.

During the second and third week like a chain gang armed with shovels, we started our attempt to dig ten footing trenches, two feet deep by two feet wide over a total distance of two thousand feet, on fallow farmland. In the middle of a drought, the ground was like concrete. After the equivalent of six full working days on site, our full team of ten people had completed just one footing...little reward for such soul-destroying hard work. With nine footings left, at this rate it would take a total of sixty days to dig them out. Morale dropped instantly, even at this early stage. Bill, recognising the signs, took the pragmatic decision to seek help. Armed with money collected from his desperate self-build team, he disappeared. We leant on our shovels (as proper manual workers do). Soon, the cavalry arrived, two yellow JCBs, expert men at the helm. We did not ask where they had come from; after all, with many police officers in our group such a question could have been counterproductive! By the end of the day, the 'contract workers' had excavated the footings for every house. The next weekend we started laying the foundations. We were now on our way. The building inspector approved the work, triggering an additional loan from the council. Alex started laying bricks.

## The Early Career with 3M

Located at Edmund House, Newhall Street, Birmingham, the 3M Midland regional office housed managers, secretaries and administrative staff. Everyone used Christian names, irrespective of status. In the police, two pips or more meant addressing the person 'sir,' so coming to terms with such familiarity did not rest easy. Whilst the American way appeared more relaxed, female secretaries sat outside the largest offices, oversized identification-plates making the bosses importance obvious. Males dominated the management structure, aping the rest of the company. The culture though, allowed repartee and jocularity. It seemed employees were contented with their lot.

During the month of training, I found it tough to digest selling methods, preferring instinct to methodology although the 'mystery opening', the 'hard and soft close', did make sense. Several older representatives, sceptical an ex-policeman could **sell**, often chided 'once a copper always a copper.' A London-based trainer did have a major influence though. Glyn Davies, a large jovial Welsh rugby international with one cap. I provocatively commented on this to a fellow compatriot of his.

"One cap! Is that all?"

The curt indignant response did not surprise.

"A Welsh cap is worth ten English."

Glyn's ability to cut to the chase demanded attention. During the two day course we discussed all aspects of managing a territory; planning the route, researching the call, building relationships, keeping records, managing accounts; very little about how to sell.

Learning the constructions of ninety self-adhesive products, their added value and the competition proved challenging but my enthusiasm never let up. Norman agreed I could spend a day on territory and suggested a visit to Charles B a buyer at Rubery Owen would be appropriate. In a new green Vauxhall

Viva company car, I drove the 30 miles to Darlaston, with confidence. On entering his office, Charles aggressively asked, without the normal courtesies, if 3M would sell to his company direct. Confirming the 3M tape philosophy of dealing through distribution, did little to impress him. With a stern blank look, he said I was wasting his time and asked me to leave. He ignored all my protestations. A disaster of a call smacked of a set up. Norman said I would have learned little from an easy one!

It is debatable whether being 'thrown in at the deep end' is an astute training philosophy, as uncertainty entered my previously positive psyche, though in a curious way it made me more determined to succeed. The last days in the office involved making telephone appointments (or trying to) with existing customers who I thought might want to see their new, fully qualified regional 3M tape salesperson. I knew all the technical details of the product range, taken on board a few techniques, so in my mind I was ready.

## Out and About Selling

Maintaining existing business, building new sustainable sales through excellent customer relations became my mantra. By implementing a soft, no pressure strategy in offering the right tape for the job and problem solving, I hoped to obtain product specifications, making the 'Scotch' turnover less vulnerable to competition. I hoped this proposition combined with my commitment to provide on-going service, would prove irresistible. Energetically, I toured the territory, making cold calls, honouring the appointments. Three days, twenty-five calls later, I was in fishing terms, 'water wacked,' lots of potential, no catch. On the next day, this all changed. Managing to solve an annoying costly cushioning problem at a major window manufacturer, I received my first ever order... five thousand 'Scotch' bumper buttons.

A pattern soon emerged. Every Friday afternoon I would plan the next five working day calls, seeking two or three firm appointments per day, to reduce the need to make soul-destroying cold calls. Active on territory by 9am, finishing between 5pm – 6pm, the selling environment seemed strange at the start. It mainly involved driving around, a boot full of samples, accompanied continuously by three large black binders supposedly containing every potential account on territory, then getting lost when searching for premises, no longer in existence though still flagged in the records. Having the obligatory brief case ready to demonstrate instantly, the wonders of my offer, only to face bored receptionists, prepared to demonstrate their importance in determining your fate. Returning home in the traffic without even a sniff at an order. More downs than ups.

It did not take a rocket scientist to know the well-dressed individuals inside cruising cars were sales representatives. Rarely when in reception areas would conversations take place between company agents. Caution abounded for fear of competitors learning something to their advantage. I treated everyone with suspicion. Yes, once a copper always a copper! There were other parallels with my previous occupation. Enduring a relatively lonely existence...interacting with many different types of people...handling efficiently any issues which arise...the excitement of achieving an objective...handling disappointment. I had been convinced police training would help rather than hinder and at this early stage evidence indicated this would be the case.

Easily making eight to ten calls per day (colleagues struggled to make six); I began obtaining significant new orders. Customers appeared to admire the endeavour involved in the self-build project, often enquiring as to progress, creating a personal as well as commercial bond. I also benefited from the backing of Castle Packaging, a wholesaler based in Walsall. We did not see eye-to-eye on everything, as I often felt they took 3M for granted, but together we built a formidable business.

Subsequently, many months later with confidence high, I telephoned Charles at Rubery Owen and on this occasion took the lead by telling him what he wanted…3M would be prepared to deal with his company direct. I drew to his attention to the benefits he was losing by not ordering from Castle Packaging…identical price, twenty-four hour local service, smaller orders. Recognising the potential gains, Charles then dropped his objection to dealing with distribution by placing a large order for 'Scotch' tape. This turnaround in fortune certainly impressed Norman as he finally confessed, with some reluctance, that he had never taken any orders from the company when he called upon them. I saw this as a significant marker. If I could break into a competitive stronghold, where my boss had failed, then perhaps I had a reasonable chance of succeeding.

Although achieving a significant sale to Rubery Owen, I failed to register even an interest at others…a packaging company being the classic. As per 'top tips' advice, I circumnavigated reception, casually walking into the factory, seeking the production manager. A worker pointed in the direction of a large office. As I knocked on the open door, a man sitting behind a desk writing, failed to stir. Hoping for acknowledgement, I moved slowly toward him. He continued to scribe. Feeling trapped, embarrassed, I started to talk to his head describing the benefits 'Scotch' tape could bring his company. He suddenly looked up, in a loud voice chastising me for entering without an invite. He refused to listen to any explanations or smooth overtures. With a strong barrage of choice words, he pointed in the direction of the exit. Tail between legs I departed hurriedly. Subsequent visits proved equally fruitless, the receptionist blocking every move. Not a good case study. At the start, this type of rejection would lead to self-analysis, but with experience, I learned to move on regardless, a vital skill in a salesperson's armoury.

Norman proved, as anticipated, to be an excellent manager, constantly providing reassurance and encouragement. I tried hard not to let him down, mindful of the criticism he would attract if I failed. An accomplished raconteur, he enjoyed sitting with his staff, his photographic memory enabling him to recount detailed facts of his two favourite subjects, sport and politics, making conversation interesting, if a little one sided on occasions. A supporter of Aston Villa, in his youth he played high quality football and cricket. He also spoke fluent Russian (truly). A fascinating, talented person.

## A Labour of Love

The self-build group progressed in accord with expectations. The skilled members were reasonably tolerant with the wide-eyed inexperienced would be builders. Bill the rough diamond foreman, lived handy to the site. His coarseness, whilst never personal, put a few noses out of joint. We were fortunate to have a very resourceful secretary, Ron the police sergeant, later to become an inspector. We had heard of other similar groups taking five years to finish the construction and two to finalise the paper work. Seven years of interest payments would be financially crippling so Ron developed a plan to minimise build time and ensure a seamless operation. Allow him to concentrate on secretarial and procurement responsibilities. Employ Alex, to lay bricks for forty hours a week (in addition to his self-build commitment) until the erection of every shell, at the rate of pay he would enjoy elsewhere. Ron estimated that if all went well, we could finish building and tie everything up in two to three years, the savings in interest offsetting the money borrowed to pay Alex a salary. It seemed merely a dream but the possibility existed. The plan received approval.

Alex, a master of his trade could lay eight hundred bricks a day. Keeping pace with what seemed his unreasonable demands proved challenging for a protected species, as I never really mastered the art of climbing a ladder with the triangular metal holder full of bricks on the shoulder...the hod.

*A brick hod is a three-sided box for carrying bricks or other construction materials, often mortar. It bears a long handle and is carried over the shoulder. A hod is usually long enough to accept 4 bricks on their side, however, by arranging the bricks in a chevron fashion, the number of bricks that may be carried is only limited to the weight the labourer can bear and the unwieldiness of that load. Typically 10-12 bricks might be carried.*

*Source: Wikipedia*

Alex needed continual supply of his raw material to function at full capacity, but hampered by incessant shoulder bruising, I struggled to carry eight bricks in the implement. Very vocal in his demands he gave no credence to inexperience, lambasting everyone around if there was any delay in supply.

Morale was high. We were building to schedule, progress clear to see, every finished shell a milestone toward completion. Materials arrived on site, just in time, Ron's fantastic organising ability to the fore. We also enjoyed the odd bonus along the way. A lorry loaded with bricks arrived on site, the driver enquiring if he had accessed a Bryant's location. We fully expected him to reverse once advised where to go, but he had other ideas. Waving his hand like a conductor mumbling obscenities, he proceeded to activate the hydraulics, dumping his load on our site. The driver ignored our protestations. Our group now owned a stack of bricks (suitable for internal walls) and he received a precious autograph. Early on, it became obvious the building trade operated its own ethical set of rules. I had so far seen two major examples. Taking the JCBs off-site to excavate the footings and a driver knowingly depositing his goods on the wrong site, merely wanting 'proof of delivery'. Sadly, these examples were trivial compared to the machinations encountered with a council official.

Insertion of the below ground drainage system was scheduled for completion during the first winter. However, continuous rain turned the site into a quagmire causing trenches to collapse and pipe collars to crack under pressure from the atmosphere. We repeatedly made good problem areas, taking advantage of any break in the weather to call in our clerk of the works. Without his approval, we could not progress, but on three separate occasions, he found fault, meaning we had to start the process again. Given that Bill deemed the drains passable, such rejection seemed illogical.

Bill explained the apparent inconsistency.

"It's obvious what is happening."

He pointed his finger at high-rise flats.

"I am a clerk of the works for that building and have refused to pass the tenth floor."

"Why?"

"Because my front drive needs repairing."

The penny dropped.

On the official's next visit, with the problem sorted, he went away, inspected the drains and signed the approval. This is difficult to justify I know, but we were not seeking approval for shoddy work, rather a recognition that when all else fails, you have to abide by an accepted practice if you want to progress, especially in our circumstances. The episode did not repeat.

With few exceptions, group members lacked the skills and experience necessary to ensure consistent workmanship. Typically, most learning occurred on the job. The first residence, situated on a corner with public paths at the front and one side became, in effect, the show house. In spite of likely residual problems, Mary and I hoped to win this accommodation during the drawing of lots, as this provided an early opportunity to have our own space again. On the evening in question, tensions of expectation were high. We drew the fourth dwelling, comfortably placed in the middle of the Sheepclose Drive cul-de-sac, which under normal circumstances would have been perfect had we not wanted to move quickly. We decided to approach the lucky owners of number one, to see if they would swap. Our simple proposition...the fourth dwelling would experience less teething problems.

We were delighted when after due consideration, he and his wife agreed. We could now look ahead positively, safe in the knowledge we would soon be able to give Mom and Jack their home back.

## Incentive Success

Morphing each week from a scruffy hard working labourer to a sophisticated well-dressed salesperson (in my mind) needed mental adjustment but I was determined to succeed at both. After six months employment with 3M, the tapes division introduced a national incentive, based upon new orders for specific products over a three-month period. My first competition, I wanted to make an immediate impression by finishing in the top three. To do so, would not only raise my credibility but also mean four days in Paris with Mary, all expenses paid. I devised a basic strategy...concentrate on a few large accounts that would make a difference. Cannon Industries, Wednesbury, a large manufacturer of white goods, secured parts to washing machines, cookers and sealed cartons with large quantities of competitive tape. Overtures to the buyer proved unsuccessful. However, the production supervisor revealed recent problems with the adhesive levels of their current product. He agreed to test the 3M alternatives, within two months specifying 'Scotch' tape, committing to a twelve-month contact. I knew the size of this order, combined with many smaller ones, would put me in a good position, but I wanted to make sure. On the last day of the contest, I got lucky, when an account with whom I had been working in Fradley, Tamworth, placed a substantial automatic box-sealing machine order plus an annual supply of tape. Seven days later, Norman rang, advising I had won in a canter.

Later, with the two other winners and their wives, we spent four days in Paris. A marvellous trip, dinner on the first floor of the Eiffel Tower, watching a great show at the Moulin Rouge the highlights. Winning this national event proved I could compete with those more experienced. Equally important, we were now starting to enjoy the fringe benefits.

After attending a couple of training courses on presentation techniques (an important part of corporate life) positive feedback indicated I had sufficient ability to keep an audience interested and awake (well at least for a couple of minutes). Chosen to represent my region during 3M competitions proved an excellent opportunity for a new young sales professional to make his mark with company executives and my twenty-day territory plan, designed to ensure effective geographic coverage became a recommended model following one of these events.

With sufficient income now to consider investing in decent clothes, I purchased several made to measure suits at reasonable prices, supplied by a superb tailor, the favourite of 3M salespeople. A charming distinguished proud man, he suffered from Parkinson's disease, yet seemed calm when touching his beloved cloth, enabling him to produce a product the envy of those who purchased elsewhere.

## First House

The plan to employ Alex proved a masterstroke. On completion of each shell, the group would move in mob handed, focusing on all the jobs necessary to finish the house. Incredibly, ten months after that dreadful first weekend, Mary, Steve (now twenty months old) and I, moved into our new Marston Green home.

The three bedroomed house with a large lounge, kitchen/dining room, provided a luxury not previously experienced. There were problems though. The lights in the kitchen only worked from a switch in the living room and vice-versa. Considering the scheme's 'electrician' had not performed such a duty for fifteen years, we were lucky to have escaped that lightly!

For a self-build group to have progressed so well over such a short period was remarkable. The press attended the footing celebration, this photograph appearing in the local newspaper. Secretary Ron is standing on the footpath. Alex the bricklayer is second from the left. Foreman Bill did not attend site that day, no doubt supervising the finish of his drive!

We were now living on a building site. At an early age, Steve could recite ten nursery rhymes and put together an intelligible sentence, to the disbelief of all who heard him. Friends warned we should prepare for the day he would swear, suggesting we ignore him when he did so. When two years old, yes two, sitting on the kitchen ledge he peered out of the window, proudly pointing.

"Look at that f------g mud dad!"

Surprised at hearing my charming young son utter such words, I ignored our friend's advice, asking him to repeat what he had said in the presence of Mary. He duly obliged, exposing a great example of parenthood and the disadvantage of living on a building site.

## Excitement on site

On completion of another residence, a new family would move in, our small community starting to take shape. One evening several of the group, having consumed a few drinks, started playing an Ouija board. A new experience, I found it hard, as did others, to keep a straight face, as the cup moved across the board. Logically, collective pressure not supernatural activity stimulated the movement. Slowly though, scepticism began to disappear. Something was happening but the possibilities were not easy to comprehend. At the end of the evening, uneasy, I vowed never to indulge again. However, Ron the secretary could not resist the temptation to play again. With his wife and two children, he spent a whole evening 'testing' the efficacy of the messages they were apparently receiving, blindfolding family members to avoid manual manipulation of the cup. The

pattern of messages convinced them, they were in the presence of a hitherto unknown family relative, who had lost his life years earlier in a mining accident. Instead of coming onto the site the following day, Ron dashed to Stoke and found that he did indeed have a relative who died in an underground explosion. He emotionally conveyed this amazing story in the site caravan on his return. Like me, he said never again. I wonder.

It was the responsibility of all concerned to keep the working tools clean. One evening in February, I found the mixer firmly cemented to the ground. Unable to break the bond with a hammer, I applied leverage to a rear wheel with a scaffolding pole. Arm strength had no effect, so I threw body weight into the fight, until a massive lightening type pain flashed across the small of my back. I fell to the ground in agony. After two weeks rest, I resumed on site, stiff, aching. Rules were in place to 'sack' anyone who did not perform to the level required. I certainly did not want to face such an ordeal.

Regretfully, a police colleague faced this unfortunate scenario. Doubling as a self-taught plumber, he consistently failed to register the required hours despite several warnings. A written complaint from a group member, advocated he should leave. This, of course would have grave consequences for his family but on the other hand, the success of the group demanded that all contribute equally. At an emergency meeting, the offender offered sincere apologies for falling behind without reasonable cause. Fighting hard to maintain his position, he promised to make up the sixty missing hours and guaranteed his future commitment. I believed him, his plea compelling, but there was a tasty offer on the table, which complicated the matter. A fully-fledged plumber had offered a lump sum equivalent to the value of the work completed so far, to join the group. The financial and skill gain for the scheme was immensely attractive; but could we in all conscience; deprive a family of a house, for individual gain. With tensions high, the secret ballot went in favour of the existing member by the smallest possible margin. For the record, I voted to keep him in the group. I believe in the notion, what goes around comes around and he deserved another chance, since he and his wife were so kind when they agreed to swop plots, so that Mary and I could move in first! Thankfully, thereafter he kept his word, becoming a perfect worker.

## The Wind Up

Remarkably, after twenty-four months of punishing toil, the self-build scheme wound up, three years ahead of similar initiatives, a phenomenal accomplishment. It spoke volumes for the organisation, commitment and skill of all concerned but in particular Ron, the secretary for his mastery of administration, procurement and the mysterious skills necessary to facilitate such a prompt orderly completion.

All scheme members, finished with a desirable property costing £2635 (£1800 material and running costs, £835 to purchase the freehold). The shrewd decisions worked well, there were few distractions and while I did not agree with everything, in the end we got the job done, the blend of skilled technicians and labourers working well. We were now on the property ladder, the location perfect. Eight miles from both parents, fifteen miles to Marion and Peter, thirty minutes from my sales territory.

Estate building work continued, the shopping centre officially opened by the Queen in April 1971. The area looked immaculate, especially the areas of mud and dirt, sprayed green for the occasion! Of the sixteen thousand houses, 80% were designated public housing. As private owners, we were a small but happy minority. In 'People Like Us' a history of the estate, WorcsAzul provides an interesting perspective.

*"There were also a range of lovely subways to navigate the busy roads and of course a number of posh sorts living in our midst in self-build houses."*

## Simon is Born

On 14 November 1968 whilst visiting Cannon Industries in Wednesbury, a call arrived. I dashed home to find Mary in labour. I declined the invitation from the midwife to attend the birth, not wanting to see my wife in pain. I did not have to wait very long before hearing our second born, Simon, enter the world, three weeks premature and weighing 7lb 2oz. Mary had been in labour for all of ninety minutes! Not long after, flowers arrived from the production manager at Cannon Industries, a generous, thoughtful gesture. Simon slept well on his first night and from a month old, ten hours was normal. He consumed baby rice in his last evening bottle when only ten days old. Not a demanding child he contentedly played on his own or with his brother. We never had any worries, except when two-years-old, he fell into the fishpond in his grandfather's garden and had to be, okay I will say it, fished out. He took his time learning to speak, bright enough to let Steve do all the talking (and swearing) for him!

## Never Going Back

I finally decided to stay with 3M after twenty months consideration. The decision had not been easy. I missed the camaraderie, buzz and prestige of the police service but enjoyed the sales environment, rewards, fringe benefits and salary at 3M. The option to retire at forty-nine-years-old with a police pension as opposed to the likelihood of eleven years longer with 3M weighed heavily, but in the end, the persuading factors were the sociable hours and the personal growth potential with a multi-national. Before making the decision I had received assurances that if all went well and with more experience, I had the potential to move into sales management. I did not want to be a career salesman.

## Mom's Happy Marriage

On 17 November 1969, Jack became my legal stepfather when he married my mother, now officially Mrs. Ridgers.

A millstone lifted, they now started a new phase in their life, thereafter happier than they had ever been, enjoying the sanctity of marriage rather than living together 'in sin'. I thought Mom's journey might have been unique. Not so. Hidden away in a BBC archive this story written by a local journalist.

*'Anna Bloomfied fell in love with her partner Bill in the 1950ies, but his first wife refused to give him a divorce.*

*"I knew we couldn't get married, but I thought it would be nice to live together and Bill wanted to so that's when we moved in together. I'd changed my name, we also moved somewhere else so no-one knew we weren't married, we were Mr and Mrs. For twenty years we lived a lie."*

*Their daughter was eighteen years when she finally found out. They married twenty years later.'*

## Life is Full of Incidents

After two-and-a-half years with 3M, I gained a small promotion to field sales trainer. Norman by this time had relocated to the London head office after promotion, Don taking his place as my boss.

The newly created role, a sign the company had confidence in my potential to move into management, had no direct authority, but it gave me the ability to influence the way in which colleagues approached their selling responsibility. Spending two days a week mentoring colleagues, three days a week on a reduced sales territory created considerable welcome variation. Working with well-established representatives, many of whom were at Norman's party, created an interesting dynamic, but they handled my involvement extremely well. They accepted that learning from a different skill base, might enhance their technique and earning power. I sought their agreement for the ideas promoted and this respectful approach seemed to work.

During this period, two traffic incidents could have had critical consequences. In Penn Road, Wolverhampton, a vehicle smashed into the side of my company car after ignoring a stop sign. Knocked unconscious for a short period, I received treatment at the local hospital. The eighty-five year old driver, subsequently pleaded guilty to careless driving.

The second incident happened, on a rainy evening at about 6pm. Whilst manoeuvring the company car into a right hand turn, I stupidly cut slightly across the corner markings allocated to vehicles exiting. In doing so, I failed to see a police motorcyclist in full uniform on his 650cc monster coming directly at me! With a collision inevitable, he threw himself off the bike. He rolled over repeatedly (a bit like a footballer trying to get his opponent sent off) as the motorbike skidded on its side to a halt under the front wing of my car. I sat numb, motionless. What had I done? The officer, uninjured, slowly brushed the dirt off his once immaculate uniform staring angrily in my direction, making it clear, by hand movement that he wanted the car window wound down. He let forth.

"You are for the high jump. Don't move a f------ inch."

A broken future flashed before me. After disqualification, how would 3M react? What would Mary say? Intrigued pedestrians stood around. Several police cars, blue lights flashing suddenly appeared as if from nowhere, making the landscape more like a major crime scene. The motorbike officer, impatient for the big chief to arrive, declined to talk...he had said all he needed to say. Standing alone, I panned around hoping to see a friendly face but spectators looked away rather than catch my eye. Suddenly, a person broke ranks enquiring if I was the driver of the car involved. At last, a sympathetic ear and maybe if local, a cup of tea. I told him my side of the story, expecting an 'arm around the shoulder' sympathetic response. Instead, he said.

"You're right in the shit aren't you?" before moving off without saying another word.

Thanks for nothing. Nevertheless, he knew his onions...I was in the mire.

A police inspector arrived. After speaking first to the motorcyclist, he directed other officers to take measurements and get the traffic flowing again. Pulled from under the car, the bike seemed relatively unscathed. The officer glared as I returned to my vehicle, following permission to leave the scene. Head swimming, I drove very slowly to the local nick, about half a mile away, thinking of the potential consequences...the reports, the explanations, the court appearance, the very real danger I would lose my licence. You know trivial things like that! After a ten minute wait in reception, the senior officer arrived. Following a caution, I gave an honest assessment of the accident admitting culpability, adding in mitigation, there were no injuries merely superficial damage to both vehicles. Tongue in cheek, I expressed the opinion that had an officer not been involved, a caution would probably be the correct action. He then said he recognised me. After discussion, it emerged we had competed against each other two years previously in a football match. Apparently, that day we beat Warwickshire Police 1-0 and I performed well. He finished the meeting by saying a decision would take at least two weeks. I left, chastened by events, fearful of the potential outcome.

Ten days after the incident, called to the local station, I anticipated prosecution for careless driving. To my relief the inspector advised a caution had been authorised. Whilst I was happy at the outcome, the motor cyclist did not let the matter drop. For three days, he waited adjacent to the house, astride his 650cc motorcycle in full uniform and as I left for work, followed my car for five miles before peeling away, the intentions of his blatant intimidation clear. I gave him no reason to pull me over but felt a little pang of conscience. He did not in the end, have his 'pound of flesh' but, had he not thrown himself off the motor bike avoiding injury, the outcome would have been far more calamitous.

Whilst escaping the car incident relatively unscathed, my lumber problems escalated, painful spasms more regular. The normal recommendation of rest and painkillers made no difference, so ultimately the local doctor referred me to Radcliffe Hospital in Oxford. The bizarre solution…completely immobilise the lower back for ninety days. On arrival at the plaster room, a nurse, who I knew well, explained the procedure.

"With a colleague we will wrap a wet bandage around your naked body from under your armpits to your hips."

She then cheekily asked if I could control myself. I answered, as you would expect, in the affirmative with a wink.

I stood nude, arms out to the side, holding onto an 'n' shaped frame as if on a cross. Although now totally exposed, I felt in control. The nurses started to pass the wet material to each other, building layers, smiling a little as they did so. We chatted innocently as the swathing continued, until the front nurse, nonchalantly as if by mistake, started to brush my private parts every time she received the bandage from her colleague. Not wishing to face the possible consequences, my thoughts moved to cars, sport, getting a large order from a customer, anything. The strategy failed however as I became aware of my appendage trying to rise from its slumber. Luckily, they finished their duties just in time and it went back to sleep. The nurses thought the whole episode hilarious. So did I.

The cold damp plaster ensured little sleep on the first night, extra blankets failing to compensate. With such heavy bulk and upper body immobility, significant adjustments were necessary in everything attempted. The 'swivel on the rump' methodology worked well to get in and out of the car, dangling feet in the bath the option for bathing. After three days, I returned to work. Astute observant customers, noticing the hidden mass, were very sympathetic. It developed into a major talking point, although of course I tried to hide the fact! Sadly, on removal of the plaster, the pain returned. Doctors said I should keep taking the pills, live with the problem.

Lying on the floor provided some relief, gentle morning exercise helping to maintain a degree of flexibility. I remained active by walking slowly, avoiding any sudden movements. The constant debilitating pain whilst annoying and uncomfortable proved manageable, but with NHS cure options limited, I tried alternative remedies. Sadly, osteopathy, heat pads, herbal pills, acupuncture, reflexology had little effect. Anti-inflammatories provided psychological hope without real benefit. Mary became an expert at doing the things necessary to keep me mobile. On one occasion, excess embrocation ran through my buttock crevice onto my testicles, the effect immediate. They stung like hell. Mary rushed to the kitchen, arriving back with a bowl of warm water. Without delicacy, I plunged the tender bits over the edge of the bowl, into the soothing $H2O$. Slowly, very slowly, normality returned, dignity restored. With humility, I can advise the event did not have any lasting effect, though it did occur to me years later, that it could have been a plot to reduce my manhood, but I dismissed the idea as fanciful!

## Chris is Born

On 25 November 1970, Jim a sales colleague with whom I had been working was due to stay at Hotel Wilkins. When we left that evening, to play snooker in Yardley, there were few signs that Mary would give birth. An hour later, at about nine, the steward of the club rushed over to our table advising that Mary had phoned to say she was in labour. Jim and I were level at the time, playing the last frame of three. With a shilling riding on this last game, we made the decision to play on, planning to blame our lateness on traffic. Fifteen minutes later, the game over, we decided to have one last drink before leaving.

I am joking of course. We left immediately after the news. Arriving home after a twenty-minute drive, the midwife had everything prepared, Mary already bearing down. Christopher completed the family at 11pm, a mere ninety minutes after the start of labour. On this occasion, I attended the birth and witnessed a wonderful, never to be forgotten experience. What a fool I had been to turn down the opportunity to see the birth of his siblings. Jim slept on the couch that night, sending a small gift to Mary the following day.

Chris, loveable and cheeky was a little more excitable than his brothers. After a period where he would scream continually if bored, he soon developed a very sunny disposition, becoming an adorable lovable child.

## An Important Promotion

After eighteen months as a field trainer, promoted to National Supervisor, New Product Development, I relinquished all territory responsibility. This newly created role involved developing opportunities for innovative untried products emanating from 3M laboratories and Norman Deakin, now working from the head office in London as the tape division national sales manager, became my boss again. Now entitled to a higher-level company car I chose a sporty model... a new Ford Capri, yellow with a black roof. Little did I realise this created disquiet with some colleagues. After spending such a short period on territory, I now had a bigger, faster car than many of them. Some, not all, felt aggrieved. Things were happening quickly. We moved (after four years in the self-build house) to  a larger three bedroom detached residence in Burnside Gardens, Walsall, putting the £3000 profit made on the sale, as a deposit. Situated on a small estate, it needed quick remedial work in the corner of the master bedroom, where soaking floorboards reeked with the stench of stale urine. Within a month, having also improved the kitchen and living room, it began to feel like home.

The new position involved continual exposure to the big chiefs, none more imposing than Bill, the divisional director. He oozed magnetic power and when he walked into a room, people took notice. Staff treated him with utmost caution wary of his ruthless reputation. My original encounter occurred on the balcony of his hotel room overlooking the Clifton Suspension Bridge, Bristol, at a pre-dinner drinks party. After making uncomplimentary comments about a particular boss, he requested my input. I felt his appraisal unfair and told him so. Bill said nothing.

## Converted Products

Unexpectedly, I received a phone call from Bill after only six months in the new product job, asking me if I would accept a position as national sales manager for the Converted Products part of his business. Working directly for him, it represented a massive promotion so without any real thought, I immediately accepted. It was a no-brainer as it also meant that in a single step I would avoid all the interim regional supervisor positions. It was rare for other than general marketing managers to report directly to a director, so in creating the structural anomaly, Bill was placing enormous faith in my ability. No pressure then!

It was rumoured the 3M Board had intended to wind up the loss making enterprise before Bill called their bluff by offering to buy it. Sensing they may have made a misjudgement, the Board rejected his offer, challenging him instead to turn the venture around in the next twelve months. While this might have been apocryphal, my appointment was not. Bill, apparently impressed, after our 'chance meeting' on the balcony, thought I would be the right person to motivate the sales team. I wondered if other seasoned managers had turned down the opening, as it seemed illogical to appoint a person with so little experience. Although a fantastic opportunity, I recognised that failure had the distinct possibility of destroying a burgeoning career.

This promotion involved working from 3M head office, Wigmore Street, London, where my final job interview took place. Hence, four months after moving in, we sold our Burnside Garden dwelling to a very likeable young couple (at £2000 above our purchase price). To find suitable affordable accommodation in the south of England, we considered locations up to forty miles from London. The place of Jack's birth, Reading, Berkshire, seemed ideal; north of the capital, convenient for visiting Birmingham with the added benefit that several of his relatives still lived in the area. We moved into a three-bedroom link detached residence, 22 Churchill Crescent, Sonning Common, Reading, a rural village with excellent amenities and schools. At prices 25% more expensive than the

Midlands, our borrowings increased overnight by £8000, the mortgage company only making an offer after seeking confirmation from 3M of my likely future earnings. Financially we were below the breadline. I kept thinking of the philosophy proffered by my new boss.

"If you can afford a dwelling don't buy it. It is not expensive enough."

He believed that a mortgage stretch at the start would soon be easily affordable by upwardly mobile staff because of the expected regular and above inflation increases. He needed to be correct otherwise we were in trouble.

Our fourth 3M move in six years was particularly tough. For the first time we were living a considerable distance from our immediate family. Although a shock to the system, we soon settled with Mary's ability to cope with both motherhood and an ambitious husband being the key factors. As usual, she took it all in her stride ensuring there would be no trace of boxes or clutter within a week of moving in. Quite remarkable. The house comprised a garage, three bedrooms, large living room, bathroom and a good-sized kitchen which overlooked an unusual and never to be forgotten garden patch. The bottom part, so steep as to be unmanageable. The top grass part, small, flat with a most monstrous drainage system protruding eight-inches above the ground level. Perfectly round, five feet in diameter, it served as the junction for all the smaller drains in the vicinity, the size providing easy worker access. The previous owners had expertly camouflaged the drain by erecting a small wall around the circumference, filling with soil and introducing flowers. I should have left well alone, because in an effort to change the configuration I demolished the wall, to reveal the monster. Impossible to reduce in size, I did the next best thing, painting everything above ground a dark green to match the grass! Cunning or what?

Not sure the boys enjoyed the green garden feature restricting their playing options, but they settled in quickly, schooling

close by. On the few occasions Mary and I were away, Jack and Mom would travel to Reading to care for the children. Returning from our first trip, the boys aged two to six years, stood welcoming at the front door, dressed identically. Simon's outfit cut him in half, shorts clinging like lederhosen, whilst those worn by Chris swamped the poor fellow. The boys adamant they were not wearing

141

each other's attire, refused to correct the obvious mistake prior to our arrival. The clothes had come from their assigned drawers (mother inadvertently putting them in the wrong place) and that was that. Steve no doubt felt very smug in his made to measure kit!

Travelling to London by train proved beyond my pocket, so I chose instead to drive to the Slough Central exit off the M4, meet with a colleague at the Holiday Inn and travel in one car for the rest of the journey. I would leave at 6.45am and arrive in London at 8am, assuming no problems. Traffic build-up made the return journey more problematical, so working until 6.30pm became normal.

Converted Products produced bespoke self-adhesive printed or die-cut tapes to customer specification. Expectations were high. Reverse the 20% decline in revenue seen over the previous eighteen months, with a team of two seasoned regional managers and twelve reps. Bill, spoke plainly.

"If we do not do this, the enterprise will cease to exist."

A case of sink or swim did not feel particularly good, but having courted senior responsibility, I could not complain. After visits to existing and potential customers, I concluded the problem was down to a tired, lazy, poorly trained and de-motivated sales team. My two direct reports blamed the product range, which came as no surprise given they had for the past ten years managed the sales teams. Twenty-year employees, they lacked any spark to motivate, their lack of vision and perspective a major limiting factor. I was angry on discovering they earned a higher salary than I did, but new in the job, with no proven record of accomplishment at this level, unaware of company compensation policies, I decided for the time being, to keep my own counsel.

Options were limited. The luxury of introducing new sales staff did not exist. Over-generous appraisals removed the possibility of moving people out. A pragmatic approach seemed the only option. From the existing team I appointed a field trainer, held an inaugural national conference and introduced a new incentive rewarding creativity. I enthused about the potential, set clear objectives and worked in the field on a regular basis. Within three months, sales picked up, thereafter continuing to improve. The sales team were now earning bonus. The two regional managers went along with the plans but I never felt certain they fully accepted an inexperienced ex-copper could bring benefit to the national position.

Bill left me alone, more or less. He had other bigger fish to fry, but during one of our infrequent conversations, I asked for confirmation that he was happy with my performance. His terse response, tended to confirm his reputation.

"You still have your job, don't you?"

Four weeks previously, he had stunned everyone by demoting three of his senior older executives. Questioning his logic, he said he believed in surrounding himself with trustworthy staff, able to deliver agreed plans. He emphasised his point, by suggesting such changes would be worth it, even at a cost of £50,000 per displaced employee. He then revealed that the backing I had given my supervisor on the balcony in Bristol, had convinced him I could be part of his team. As I thought, it had been a test! Given he had not sacked me, taking an 'in for a penny in for a pound' approach, I warily informed him of the fact that his sales manager's salary was less than the two regional managers. My strong suggestion that he should rectify the anomaly was answered a couple of months later when I received a significant pay increase and for the first time option shares. This helped reduce the strain of paying the new 15% mortgage rate (up from 8% since moving to Churchill Crescent). We were staying ahead of the game, 3M maintaining their philosophy of rewarding high performers with above inflation increases, supplemented by improvements in the overall package.

## Health Farm

With personal financial pressures easing, the stresses of managing a 3M business started to be worthwhile. As experience grew, I felt quite capable of handling any situation. Domestically everything was fine, Mary with her customary efficiency, coping admirably with the day-to-day chores, the kids happily settled. However, the back problems continued, paracetamol having little effect. Shuffling along a corridor one day, in obvious pain, Bill enquired as to the problem. With massive sensitivity, at company expense, he booked me into Grayshot Hall Health Farm, Hindhead, Surrey, for a seven-day stay and on arrival, I parked my company car between an Aston Martin and Bentley. Expensive vehicles were everywhere. With little personal cash, I vowed to resist involvement with any person or group. With a propensity for talking, I knew this would be difficult.

Nothing much happened on the opening day. I spoke to very few people, retiring early. In the morning, breakfast arrived; cabbage leaves and water...rabbit food. My 'must be a mistake' gesture soon turned to dismay when I realised it was not an error. Later, sitting in a small surgery, the doctor emphasised the need to stick to the assigned diet to cleanse the body of all impurities. For the next thirty hours, the purgatory of not eating 'normal' food resulted in a continuous bad headache. On the third day things changed. I awoke very relaxed and subsequently enjoyed the experience of doing almost nothing. I started to enjoy a new phenomenon...chilling out.

In spite of trying to keep a low profile, I enjoyed snooker with a group of Jewish guests three nights in succession, enjoying their 'non-fattening champagne' generosity at a local pub. The next day, having no funds to reciprocate, I retired to my room early evening, instead of joining the group as usual. A knock at the door, revealed Solly (the oldest affiliate of the group) standing outside, demanding an explanation.

"I believe in paying my way. I am skint. "

"Don't worry; we take care of our own."

I looked sheepishly at him.

"I am not one of yours as I'm sure you know."

"We enjoy your company and want you to join us."

On arriving at the pub, he removed a big cigar from a case, together with his cutter. In full view of his friends, he moved the tiny implement near my trousers, simulating a snip.

"You are now one of us," he proudly announced.

The others clapped at this mock ceremony. I joined in the fun, feeling more at ease, amazed at their munificence. Smart intelligent people, a pleasure to be with, they helped to make the week a very pleasant experience. David, the biggest operator, had a trade card…'Do Anything Ltd.' He explained his philosophy.

"I will take on any job providing I can make a profit."

His entrepreneurial brain worked overtime as he outlined his new idea… surreptitiously selling sandwiches (and non-fattening champagne) to health farm residents around the country!

By the end of the week, I could casually swim fifty lengths a day. A month later, in a pool by the office, I struggled over three lengths, no doubt reflecting the strains of everyday living and a woeful technique.

## Laminectomy Relief

The health farm, whilst most enjoyable, did little to ease the back problem. The debilitating constant pain was difficult to handle. I became more irritable. Compared to many others, my situation was not too bad, but I feared the hurt would remain forever. A new doctor then changed everything.

"You are condemning me to a life of pain. I have been suffering like this for over five years."

This pathetic tear in the eye response to her solution of painkillers, must have touched a nerve. She instantly softened

146

her stern attitude, suggesting an alternative path to recovery. A few weeks later, at the Oxford Radcliffe Hospital, a specialist conducted a myelogram.

*A myelogram uses a special dye (contrast material) and X-rays (fluoroscopy) to make pictures of the bones and the fluid-filled space (subarachnoid space) between the bones in your spine (spinal canal). Source: Web MD.*

A group of doctors, in my presence, discussed the findings, the consultant advising an immediate laminectomy operation was necessary.

*A laminectomy is a surgical procedure that removes a portion of the vertebral bone called the lamina. At its most minimally invasive, the procedure requires only small skin incisions. The back muscles are pushed aside rather than cut and the parts of the vertebra adjacent to the lamina are left intact. Source: Wikipedia .*

The surgery proved to be a great success. The pain disappeared and within forty-eight hours, physiotherapists were helping my recovery. Up until this point, Mary had only driven locally, yet every day, she would make the eighty mile round trip, arriving on the ward, as if she had stepped out of a bandbox. I felt so proud to have such a beautiful wife.

A person in the bed opposite spoke with a strong Berkshire accent. His wife visited every afternoon, having travelled over an hour. Within thirty minutes or so of her arrival, he would inevitably fall asleep even though she was still at his bedside. I suggested it would be good form if he remained alert until she departed. He smiled.

"Silly bugger, she knows I doze in the afternoon. She should visit in the evening!"

There is nowt as queer as folk.

## Packaging Systems

After thirty months in Converted Products, my appointment as national sales manager of the £5 million, Packaging Systems Group, came as a complete surprise. The self-adhesive tape, machinery and dispenser product range competed in a well-inhabited market, a small constant profit proving difficult. It became apparent that sales of the high margin products were too small to compensate for low profit volume box sealing tape. The mix needed to improve. Many thought managing the mix would be impossible, but negativity did not figure in my DNA.

Working for general marketing manager Dan, I inherited a strong sales organisation. The three regional managers, open to new ideas, embraced the concept. To encourage the full participation of the twenty representatives and two engineers, I introduced a bonus scheme rewarding sales of the profitable items rather than a single turnover measure. Increased marketing spend consolidated the initiative, the whole package released at a national conference. I double worked with the entire sales team, walking the talk, reviewing progress monthly. The tough regime, not for the faint hearted, distinguished the excellent from the average. Slowly but surely the mix and profit steadily improved and consolidated 3M's position as a serious supplier to the packaging market.

## Amateur Coach, Qualified Referee

Simon joined Rotherfield United, the local junior football team, developing into a competent midfield competitive player, eventually captaining the side. I accepted an invitation to coach the team. We failed to reach the summit of the league but with an exuberant team of average ability, we reached a cup final, losing to a late goal. During this period, I qualified as a referee, officiating at many junior matches and a league final. Not accustomed to having a man in the middle, the parents now had the option of expressing their feelings toward an adult on the field instead of the opposing youngsters! I graduated to senior games but found the player's abuse incomprehensible. Little respect existed, so after five years, I resigned. The experience of playing, coaching and refereeing, provided all the necessary qualifications to be an expert pundit. I have been shouting at the television during matches ever since.

## Great Characters

Promotion from within, a strong aspect of 3M philosophy, provided competent employees with real opportunities to progress. Harold started working for the company as a groundsman (so the rumour goes) because he could also play baseball (3M looking to strengthen their UK team).

We first met when I had been with the company six months. Bronzed with a winning smile, he had advanced to the lofty position of GMM.

"Hello Terry how are you. I have heard a lot about your excellent work in Staffordshire. How are you finding selling compared to policing?"

Flattered such a prominent figure would recognise me, I went to a group of established colleagues, after he left.

"Guess what? Harold knew my name."

They smiled in response.

"Sorry to disappoint, but he actually had no idea who you were until he asked us to identify the bald headed, badly dressed man with the Birmingham accent!"

At our second meeting, he got right to the point suggesting I needed to change three things to get on.

- Lose the accent...he had a strong dialect.

- Cease wearing a leather jacket to meetings...he wore an expensive black number.

- Stop being so friendly, be more selective...yes, he often ignored people.

Interesting advice from him on high. The leather jacket had credence, not the other two.

A larger than life character, he was creature of habit. Each day he would leave his home at 7.55am precisely, be driven by his devoted wife, along an identical route to catch the 8.15am train. On reaching the station, he would give his spouse a peck on the cheek and depart the car silently. This routine was so ingrained, that a male colleague, driving him instead of his wife, also received an instinctive kiss. When told what had happened, Harold merely shrugged his shoulders.

He would stand in an identical spot on the platform every day, in order to board the carriage nearest the driver. This would normally allow him to sit in the middle of a bench seat, unhindered by any other passenger. However, on one occasion, uninvited commuters sat either side of him. Instinctively to regain space, he spread his legs and arms as wide as possible. The travellers, not wishing to upset such a dominant figure crushed themselves into what remained of their seat. Proud of his achievement, Harold peered over the top of his newspaper to find a person in a seat opposite seemingly pointing in his direction. Harold ignored such rudeness, more interested in reading how his shares had grown. Intrigued through, he glanced again minutes later, to find the man still gesturing. Harold looked down to find his flies were wide open. You cannot make this stuff up can you.

I reported to him for six months during which time he rarely spoke about business or responded to any correspondence. He routinely rejected any involvement in interviewing prospective sales representatives, though as a courtesy, I always advised him. On the second day of a long selection process, he suddenly appeared. Peering through the glass panel in my office door, he started shaking his head vigorously from side to side behind the candidate, before moving away.  With no idea why the theatrics, I stopped the interview. I found him relaxing in his office.

"Why all the head movement."

"The candidate is no good." I tried not to smile.

"You have not even spoken to him, how can you make such a judgement? Do you know him?"

"I can read the back of people's heads. He is a bad egg."

Trying to stifle a snigger, I asked sarcastically,

"Are you trained in such a skill?"

"Believe me I know what I am talking about. Take him on if you wish, but I am telling you, he is no good."

No more logic or explanation. What a character. What an enigma. From groundsman to GMM. Good at commerce and a psychic to boot! Did I employ the interviewee? Well, even though tempted to prove the absurdity of his attitude, I decided to delay any decision pending further enquiries (CID training coming in useful)! Three weeks later, purely by chance, I discovered the candidate had an appointment in court for domestic abuse! Although Harold failed to appear again during interview sessions, on a couple of occasions when undecided, I secretly hoped he would return.

The head office, a stone's throw from Oxford Street, a mere mile from Buckingham Palace was an interesting place to work. Employees seemed genuinely happy with their lot with little evidence of backbiting...well at least in the lower levels. Early evening socialising in the local pubs was normal, to avoid the dreadful traffic. A ten-hour day although tiring, never seemed a chore, the larger than life' individuals, helping to keep morale high. Malcolm, the GMM (who gave me my final interview) fitted this description admirably, his long expressive face demanding attention. After university, he formed a script-writing team with fellow graduates, Sid Green and Dick Hills, but left early, unable to live on scraps of income. His chums subsequently became legendary writers for Morecombe and Wise. Their loss, 3M's gain. A born showman, we all turned to him at any function, to provide the entertainment. He would normally acquiesce. His act, a mixture of standard rugby type banter and observation humour never failed to produce tears of laughter. His 'near the knuckle' light-hearted style, presented with a twinkle in his eye, rarely offended. At dinner with ten distributors in a private room, discussion started about the war. He arose from his chair, running round the room, acting as a pilot, receiving instructions from the ground. At a function in Marbella, he suddenly breezed onto a crowded dance floor dressed in white, pretending to conduct a jive with an imaginary partner. Everyone stood aside to watch him expertly manoeuvre his invisible beau around the floor. Brilliant. As we became more profitable, we started inviting paid entertainers to conferences to freshen up proceedings. In Blackpool, two female vocalists asked an audience member to join them. Predictably, Malcolm volunteered. On stage, whilst they serenaded him with a love song, his subtle face, body and leg movements mimicked the words. The experienced singers went along with his hilarious antics. The star of the evening, Roy Walker soon to be a T.V. favourite, wondered why we had employed him, with such a funny man in our midst. He had a point. What he did not know was that Malcolm was also an astute executive. The fact that such characters were not discouraged said a lot for the spirit of company. Not all the larger than life people were entertainers though. George, a dear friend with a rapier wit, served during the war as a rear turret gunner ('tail end Charlie') on military aircraft. As such, he became an instant and easy target for enemy fighter planes. Shot down three times, he twice escaped from incarceration. He was in captivity the day Churchill announced the German surrender. A modest man, he spoke infrequently of his exploits preferring to talk of the present rather than the past. A real hero.

## Happy Conferences

Such personalities within the corporate world created an enlightened atmosphere. I worked hard, played hard and tried not to take myself too seriously. Rather like Malcolm, (although nowhere near as good) I would cheerfully take the entertainment lead for the benefit of morale and group togetherness. At a sales conference in Birmingham, I attended the evening meal wearing a Beatles type wig, hoping to create humour, given my lack of hair. The compere announced.

"You will note Terry has not yet taken his place at the top table. After many years of deliberation, he has decided to wear a wig permanently. If you respect Terry, I would ask that you do not laugh when he comes in. Allow him to integrate normally."

I entered the room, with no idea what to expect. Stony silence. Not a snigger, heads turning away in embarrassment. As I sat down at the top table, a guest from America aware of the prank, stood up to save the day.

"If I looked like Terry, I think I would be tempted to wear a wig as well. But from the sublime to the ridiculous, come on!"

This broke the ice.

"Terry paid a substantial price for the wig. I suggest we pass the hat round."

The quiet hum turned to open conversation, snide smart funny comments generating laughter. The collection contained two-pound-fifty, three cigarette ends and a small I.O.U. The evening proved to be great success. The white knight from America kindly observed later, that the lack of laughter originally, resulted from respect not embarrassment!

## Conference Dilemmas

Our conferences were well organised due to Mike, a superb detailed project planner. He orchestrated everything, but incidents did happen, when out of his sphere of influence. The person who hoovered up dregs from wine glasses after everyone left (he eventually died of alcohol poisoning). The local madam, who complained there had been no takers after she sent her 'girls' to the hotel, or the occasion we thought an employee had died after finding him flat out on his bed, unconscious, the worse for wear.

Whilst, enjoying dinner with Norman in a Marbella hotel, a sales representative from the West Country staggered to our table in a drunken state, aggressively and crudely slagging-off management. Demonstrating wonderful composure Norman seemed unperturbed, but such indiscipline was unacceptable to me. At 6.30am the following morning, roused from bed, the offender agreed to resign when told he faced the sack. He caught the next plane back to the UK.

Periodically, 3M International would organise a global conference attended by country managers and vice presidents

(VPs) from the USA. At a gathering in Brussels, several coaches waited to take delegates to the event. My morning call failed to materialise. Five minutes after the scheduled departure, my room telephone rang, an executive voice making it clear my career was on the line.

"You had better get your butt down here immediately."

As I left the hotel, hurrying to board the transport, a sea of faces gawked with distain. To make things worse, with no seats available, I had to stand. Explaining the circumstances to anyone who would listen, received little sympathy. I felt like a leper, alone and in disgrace. During his opening speech, the compere did not help.

"It is the first time we have had five international VPs attend a conference of this nature and the first time Terry Wilkins has held up the traffic...well since he was a police officer that is!"

Delegates enjoyed the sarcasm. I swallowed hard. Two years later, in Minnesota, at an evening function, a VP attendee at the European conference sarcastically congratulated me after I turned up on time!

## On the Move Again

In 1975, 3M announced the employment of external consultants to examine the options for moving the UK Head Office from Central London. Eighteen months later, two directors moved into the Gatwick area. As a result, West Sussex appeared to be the favoured location. The re-location provided an ideal opportunity to move into a bigger house. It came as an unwelcome surprise therefore, when 3M officially announced

Bracknell, Berkshire, as its new head office location. A generous relocation allowance, available to those employees living more than 15 miles away from the new head office, appeared out of our reach, with Sonning Common 13.9 miles away. The postcode lottery seemed so unfair given our expectation. I asked 3M management to consider our situation and thankfully, the Board with admirable fairness, agreed to a slightly adjusted full package.

We decided the Wokingham area would best serve our family needs and quickly found a large four bedroomed pseudo Georgian dwelling in Luckley Road, a quiet residential location. Close to Bracknell with good education facilities, it appeared ideal, but the seller decided to back out at the last juncture. For the next few miserable weeks, we found that similar high standard houses were circa £10,000 more expensive (confirming the seller backed out after realising he had sold too cheaply) and out of our reach. I became disillusioned and grumpy. Mary on the other hand, fed up with such intransigence and open to more options, decided to investigate on her own.

Several days later, Mary proudly announced she had put a returnable deposit on a new house. Undaunted, she then revealed the price was £27,000. This was £3000 higher than the loan agreed by our mortgage company for the Luckley Road house. Mary seemed to be living in fantasyland, but cool as a cucumber, she addressed my obvious discomfort by revealing we were due to see a moneylender in the morning. A ballsy checkmate move. Twenty-four hours later, feeling miffed to be out of the loop until now, I stepped into the four bedroom detached in a quiet cul-de-sac, relatively disinterested. My mood soon changed though. Not overlooked, ideally situated, the house seemed to meet all our needs. The moneylender subsequently agreed to top up the Nationwide loan, at a high interest rate but thankfully, it proved unnecessary when the building society increased their loan to 95% of the asking price, after 3M (again) confirmed I was still upwardly mobile.

Selling Churchill Crescent proved arduous.   The first five couples failed to make an offer in spite of positive comments. Not slow on the uptake, we logically reasoned the massive green drain protruding above the grass on the back lawn could be the problem. Learning from the previous owners, I hastily erected a small wall around the drain, filling the monster with soil and flowers.   Remarkably, the next interested party made an offer.

Our new home at 5, Perth Close, Woodley proved ideal, two miles from the M4 and a stone's throw from Willow Bank junior school and Waingels Copse senior faculty. With seven families moving into the cul-de-sac at the same time we soon settled. Likely to be our last move for many years, we were now able to consolidate our position.

I joined the committee of Woodley Residents Association, at the suggestion of next-door neighbour Mike, the chairperson. We tackled many local issues including litter, pollution from a local factory and traffic. The idea that the giant Reading Music Festival could be re-located to a recently defunct landfill site rallied the community and the idea never gained any momentum. If to their advantage, local Councillors showed interest in our activities their deviousness and massive egos forever evident. After five years, two as Chair, I resigned to concentrate on other things.

## The Land's End

A wonderful character, Vic Appleton introduced me to The Land's End. Aptly named, the drinking hole stood at the end of a narrow country lane, a fast flowing ford restricting traffic in bad weather. Splendidly isolated, ownership drifted. That is, until Mike and Kate decided the location should be an attraction rather than a disadvantage. Moving from a local tenancy, they introduced Brakspear ales, transformed the

decoration and the clientele.

The 601 Club, started after five couples became friends. With the simple rule that everyone had to be in the pub no later than one minute past six every Friday, we became a bit of a clique, in danger of dominating the surroundings. Although other visitors may have found it intimidating to see ten people standing at the bar, joking, enjoying each other's company, I would like to think we contributed to the welcoming atmosphere. Mike and Kate, extended to each member a tab and as a courtesy on the bar cheese and roast potatoes.

For several weeks, a distinguished couple kept 'hanging around' the periphery, joining in conversations when they could. Occasionally, the man would offer to buy a drink all round. By stealth, Bernard and Barbara joined the 601 Club achieving their ambition.

"You lot seemed to really enjoy yourselves, so having recently moved into the area we wanted to join you. Persistence and bribery obviously paid off."

Vic, Sue, Ian, Carol, Nick, Pauline, Peter, Lyn, Bernard, Barbara, Mary and I were in for the long haul. We had a ball as part of the Land's End family. Five years on the trot, the group spent New Year's Eve at the pub, returning the following morning (no matter how we felt) to clear the mess.

Mike and Kate were superb intelligent tenants. They provided a safe, warm welcoming atmosphere, receiving in return a regular income with occasional free labour. If Mike thought the pub needed a lick of paint he would casually mention it and the 601 Club would soon be plying the walls with emulsion...astute or what? They were the old-fashioned type, spending much of their spare time on our side of the bar. They drank a little, smoked a lot. Many of our group accompanied them on a weekend break to the unique Rudesheim in Germany, a place full of character. An ideal pub coach trip location! Twenty-four hours spent on the coach is too long, but words uttered by Mike made it bearable. After talking earnestly to Kate, he suddenly threw his head back in exasperation, saying in a loud voice.

"Twenty years of experienced foreplay and you call it bloody fiddling!"

Kate looked disgusted. Mike never let on the reason for such a reaction.

During one year, we celebrated the birthday of every 601 Club member with a 'surprise.' For Ian, a firefighter, we all dressed up in - yes, you have guessed it - a firefighter's uniform. For Mary, I found a reason for both of us to return home five minutes after leaving. In the meantime, the gang, to whom I had provided the front door key, gathered inside dressed as Mr. & Mrs. Mop. When we arrived, they sang 'Happy Birthday' as soon as Mary recovered from the shock. For Pauline, she arrived at a restaurant accompanied by her husband Nick, to find the gang hiding - and so it went on. On the occasion of my significant day, a banner 'It's m m my 40th birthday today,' hung across the front of the house (a play on my employment with 3M). All right, it is not brilliant, but in consideration of how corny you think it might be, consider the facts. Vic and Ian the firefighter, met at a pre-determined place in the middle of the night, put two ladders against the wall, shinned up, returning to their car after attaching the sign. What would have happened if a police officer had seen them, or a neighbour? We decided to take an entirely different approach when celebrating Mike's birthday. We pretended to forget! Having arrived at the pub on the day in question, the gang left two hours later without acknowledging his special day. Mike's face expressed thunder as we departed. Having been involved in celebrating every other birthday, he expected at least a card. At 10pm, we all sneaked back into the pub and hid behind the bar. Mike was with customers on the other side, when the barman rang the bell, cue for the gang to pop up and sing a 601 special, 'The twelve drinks of Christmas.'

Mike showed his pleasure and relief, as the whole pub sang happy birthday.

I knew it would be a challenge to surprise Vic on his birthday, the last of the year. I devised a simple cunning plan...confound him twice. At 6.30am Mary and a couple of 601 compatriots banged on the ornate front door of his cottage. Sue his wife, knowingly stayed in bed. As Vic sleepily stumbled downstairs in his pyjamas, his guests sang happy birthday. Little did he know that another surprise lay in store that evening. Too convoluted to explain in detail, it entailed "stealing" his car, a police vehicle with flashing lights, a garage, a lock, a crow bar and a kilt! The involvement of outside parties, created a potential risk but it worked like a dream, although having to jemmy the lock off Mike's garage never featured in the plan! Vic, suitably impressed by the ingenuity, reciprocated by buying everyone a drink.

We began seeing a large John Player Special in the car park. On asking Mike to identify the hidden millionaire, he pointed to a follicular challenged bloke, just like me. Our introduction to Keith and Alma, soon developed into a very close friendship, in spite of the revelation that it was actually Keith's company car, not his own!

Mary and I held a 'Come as you were when the ship went down' party, a variation on fancy dress. I dressed as a punk disc jockey, Nick as a diver, Pauline as a pregnant bride - I think you get the picture. Ian warned beforehand that he would be unable to stay long in his outfit. He staggered through the living room, slacks round his ankles, wearing a thong, toilet roll in his hand. He then dressed. We were a crazy lovely crowd.

Bernard and Barbara, the experts at food preparation and presentation, held many dinner parties at their large house near Woodley shopping centre. They were fantastic generous hosts, Barbara silver service trained, Bernard an excellent chef. As well as superb food, fine wine, humour, banter, earnest conversation often took place. There were no major disagreements...except one. When we were on the cheese course, discussion focussed on the effect newspapers have on opinion forming. I cited several examples where bad publicity had rightly or wrongly, created an indelible image of a celebrity.

"Take Mary Rand. Years ago, some newspapers suggested that she was a bit of a flirt."

(For those who are unaware, she won a gold, silver and bronze medal winner in the 1964 Tokyo Olympics, becoming the golden girl of British athletics).

Bernard, sitting at the other end of the table, raised his eyebrows, his casual demeanour changing instantly.

"You have no right to say that. Mary is a lovely person."

Thinking his response merely chitchat, I continued.

"Well, I am only repeating what the papers said."

Bernard did not let up.

"It's not true," he said in a raised, angry voice.

"You cannot say that Bernard, you don't know her."

"They are not true Terry, I can tell you that. We lived next door to Mary in Henley for five years and she is the godmother of Melanie (his daughter)."

Stunned, the room went silent. I had cheekily chosen to move the debate along, randomly picking a celebrity by name, unluckily choosing a friend of the host! What are the odds? We

 had known Bernard and Barbara for years and they had never mentioned they knew an Olympic gold medallist, let alone one who happened to be almost family. Bernard graciously accepted my grovelling apology, saying I would in the future, have the chance to meet the athletic icon.

Two years later, on discovering we were due to visit America, Bernard contacted the 'golden girl' of British athletics, who now lived in California. Subsequently, accompanied by Keith and Alma, we spent three delightful hours at the residence of the Olympian and her partner in the snowy hills above Los Angeles. They met on a blind date arranged by a friend. Mary did not tell him of her fame for four months. Can you imagine the surprise?

"I need to tell you something. I am a world famous athlete. Here are my three Olympic medals!"

*An excerpt from Sporting Life*

## Rand was born to win by David Martin, PA Sport

*Mary Rand with her long blonde hair was the first "Golden Girl" of British athletics, and in Tokyo in 1964 fully justified that accolade as the first British woman to win an Olympic medal.*

*Rand - now living in the United States and looking as trim and fit as ever - will never forget the marvellous October day when she put together the finest series of long jump performances and the world record leap of 6.76 metres, which gained her the victory for which she craved. But that was not all the 24-year-old Wells-born star achieved in the first major sports championships to be held in Japan. Mary also came away with a silver in the pentathlon - also only the second ever person to exceed 5000 points - and following those exertions ran in the British 4x100m relay team which won the bronze medal.*

How ironic. By being provocative, I met a legend, who in spite of all her achievements displayed a refreshing level of humility. Gracious, immensely proud of her place in history, she never expressed envy at the earnings of today's sport stars, happy to have represented her country for the honour rather than the financial benefit. The memory will remain forever.

The group remained close for about ten years but eventually, the wonderful 601 Club fragmented into smaller friendship groups. Our Friday activity changed. Every week, Mary and I would play a Bavarian form of Canasta (do not ask) with Bernard, Barbara, Vic and Sue, rotating the venue. The hosts would provide food, the evening lasting a very pleasant 4-5 hours. Twenty-five years on, we still play on a Friday, with Keith and Alma, if diaries allow.

## General Marketing Manager

Following Dan's move to Brussels, I assumed the privileged responsibility of managing the profit and loss of a major 3M business unit. With ten years' service aged thirty-four, this promotion was beyond all my expectations. As General Marketing Manager, Packaging Systems, my office size increased considerably. A large round table with four comfortable chairs, a massive desk and two cushion padded chairs, rested on a luxurious thick carpet. On moving in, I found the centre of the curtains pinned together, with a notice, 'Punch and Judy show starts at 9am.' Superb repartee.

I continued to engage in friendly banter with all levels of staff, engaging in conversation, passing any amusing (well at least in my mind) observation that came to mind. Most responded positively, except one young marketer. He did not even smile when I commented his loud tie must have been a present! His boss, a charming witty Liverpool supporter, provided an honest appraisal.

"Terry, I didn't know you were so naive. You are now an important person with the biggest office on the floor. When you banter with him, he does not know how to react or respond. He does not know your style. So rather than making him feel good, you make him concerned!"

Rightly, this episode demonstrated I could no longer act as one of the lads. I did change, not much, but enough to create a little distance.

## The Mining Experience

During the next ten years at GMM level, I managed several key operations. Shortly after moving to Occupational Health and Safety Products (OH&SP), the National Coal Board approved a 'Scotch' disposable dust respirator, as a suitable alternative to the traditional, cumbersome, unhygienic rubber type mask. This spoke volumes for the expertise of the OH&SP staff who had worked on the project for many years. A real opportunity now existed to improve miner's health and gain profitable turnover. On reviewing the strategic plan, the lack of involvement of the National Union of Mineworkers appeared to be a weakness. A month later, at 10.30am precisely, Joe Gormley, in his trademark Crombie overcoat and dark blue brimmed hat arrived at the company flat in Grosvenor Hotel, Hyde Park. Relieving him of these outer garments exposed a cardigan with a small noticeable hole. Joe apologised saying his

wife hated sewing. He rejected the offer of coffee or tea.

"A brandy would be nice. Wherever I go in the world, I have this tipple. It's so consistent!"

We were meeting Joe during a period when constant in fighting with his deputy Arthur Scargill, often made headlines. Toward the end of the meeting, he received a call from his office.

"He is doing what? No, I'll handle on my return."

As he finished the conversation, I asked if he wanted to leave.

"No, not at all. Mr Scargill has called for a vote of no confidence in me at tomorrow's board meeting...again, but I am confident he will be defeated seven votes to six. It would be no different if I were in hospital. A vote would be taken to see if I should be sent a card and this would be carried by seven votes to six."

He paused.

"May I please have another brandy?"

How cool. In spite of the stress, certain of the unwavering loyalty from certain members of his Board, he could still relax. Newspapers later confirmed the defeat of the motion (by one vote).

Joe Gormley resigned in 1982, receiving a Peerage. Seen as the face of reason he had been involved in momentous battles with the government, winning deep respect from the likes of Ted Heath and Maggie Thatcher. He died in 1993, the nation mourning the loss of a great man. Nine years later, the BBC highlighted his patriotism by revealing he had worked for Special Branch, passing information on extremism within his Union. I am proud to have spent four hours in his company.

'Scotch' brand safety products were relatively unknown in the mining industry. The annual Coal Board exhibition in Blackpool provided the ideal occasion to spread the word. Chief Executive Sir Derek Ezra, appreciating our involvement, responded positively to a suggestion we should meet the miners in their working habitat.

On a fine day in September, with Norman Deakin and two colleagues, I visited Bates Colliery in Durham. After a safety briefing, donned in miner's equipment including of course the new 3M disposable mask, we accessed the depths via a 'cage', accompanied by two pit supervisors. It was cold, cramped, great fun, a real giggle. We then travelled for ten minutes in a small open man-rider train, before walking four-hundred yards in a rapidly dropping temperature. On reaching a solid cliff face, I relaxed thinking we would soon return to the surface to enjoy coffee. Suddenly our leader pointed to a gap at the bottom of the cliff face, two feet high, five yards wide.

"The seam runs under the North Sea. I'll lead, you all follow in sequence, and my mate will bring up the rear."

He lowered his body to an almost a horizontal position, before  propelling himself forward to vanish through the gap. We were evidentially nowhere near the coalface...our adventure had not even started. I am not good in enclosed spaces or heights, but the ramifications of refusing were not good, so using elbows and knees I scrambled under the cliff face, followed by our remaining pit guide, the chain complete. In pitch black, we inched along through three-foot square hydraulic steel canopies in the nearly prone position, a small helmet light the only comfort. Strangely, focussing on Norman's ample posterior immediately ahead provided some comfort. I silently followed, arse crawling an apt description. Coal dust nestled in the light beam, highlighting the significant potential for superior face protection that did not restrict breathing. I kept thinking of the generation of miners who in the past worked without any health and safety considerations. No wonder they died young.

Running parallel to our route on the right, a circular automatic shearer noisily pulled chunks of coal from the face onto a conveyor belt. We stopped for a breather. I twisted, arching round to ask the miner bringing up the rear.

"How far to go?"

Talking through his 3M mask (something that would have been difficult with the old rubber type) he shouted.

"Half a mile!"

After another ten minutes of crawling, all hell let loose. Without notice, over a period of fifteen seconds or so, in deafening noise, the earth began to shake viciously, the impact so great I thought it could be an explosion. Life did not pass before me, I did not panic but I was genuinely scared. Crouching alongside our tunnel, a very unconcerned miner.

"What the .... is happening?" I shouted urgently.

"Oh, nothing. This is routine. We are merely collapsing the roof of the mined out area, to relieve pressure. Have you not been told?"

"No."

Whilst, I felt a degree of comfort from this explanation, thoughts of a potential conspiracy existed.

"When the top executives from 3M arrive let's see how brave they are?"

After another thirty minutes of slow painful exhausting progress, we reached the end of the coalface, able at last to stand and stretch. I joined colleagues in a bedraggled circle, expecting to hear excited badinage about the 'earthquake' but tiredness sapped conversation. All around miners shovelled remnants of coal into low railway trucks whilst pockets of seawater cascaded through the erosions in the cave's ceiling.

On the surface after a shower, we assembled to enjoy a hot meal. Asked by the plant manager for feedback, we initially picked words carefully, until he indicated willingness to take questions.

"How can people be asked to work in such dreadful conditions?"

"Please don't feel sorry for the miners. They are the highest paid manual workers in the country and are on the coal-face no more than five and a half hours per day."

"Their health must suffer?"

"We do all we can to reduce the risk. Consider this as well. The mining tradition is within families. Ninety percent, who leave to try another job, return within twelve months. They miss the camaraderie, the money and the fact that underground, they do not have supervisors continually inspecting their work. They see big benefits in being a miner."

In discussing the merits of our product, he re-iterated the benefits. Lightweight, hygienic, disposable, better dust protection, improved safety benefits. 3M had another winner on its hands.

I would like to say the picture you see is *after* the adventure given our relaxed attitude, but you have probably gathered it happened before we knew of the discomfort to follow. Norman Deakin is second from the left, leaning casually.

The mining community gained my additional respect. I felt privileged to have inhabited their world for a short period and vowed to be more circumspect in future when voicing opinions about things I know little about.

Oh, I forgot to mention a couple of other things. At lunch, a miner with half a face and a prosthetic arm (following an underground explosion) served our table. Scary. Shut down in 1986, the site is now a large housing estate. During its fifty functioning years, thirty-three miners died underground. Unreal.

Footnote. Arthur Scargill assumed the presidency of the union when Joe Gormley finally handed over the reins. Try as I may I never succeeded in meeting him. His senior secretary acknowledged my phone calls and letters but that was it. This perhaps tells another story!

## Discectomy

In 1986, twelve years after the first operation, I started to suffer sharp knife-stabbing pains in the lower spine accompanied occasionally by massive spasm. Instinctively I knew the problem could be grievous. Needing prolonged rest, a door resting on a table became my living quarters, twenty-four seven. Alongside the new bed, slats on two louvered doors became a filing place for papers. With a telephone handy, it was business as normal - well not quite.

Mary spoke to a doctor from our local surgery. He declined to visit, advocating painkillers as usual. During this period, Vic would often visit, keeping my spirits high by sharing a drink or three. Two weeks after the start of the sojourn, whilst still lying flat, I sneezed. My body jerked unexpectedly upwards, accompanied by excruciating pain. Given the severity, Mary contacted the doctor again, receiving the same answer. Rest and painkillers. I struggled upstairs into bed, work no longer of interest. With little relief, I stopped eating, a little desperate. A move of any sort resulted in a red-hot poker pain in the lower spine. More overtures failed to induce a doctor to visit. We found it hard to fathom such an attitude. I do not cry wolf.

Four days later, unable to take any more agonising pain, Vic and I hatched a simple plan to gain the desperately needed attention. I would somehow get into his car; he would drive to a quiet spot; dump me on the side of a road; ring 999 and say he had found an injured person lying on the footpath. This would surely result in blue light transport to the nearest infirmary. However, before adopting such radical action, Mary tried the surgery once more, this time speaking to her own doctor. Her magic worked. Doctor Monger arrived quickly, contemplating the pathetic person in a pool of pain. He did not examine or touch me; he could feel the agony. An ambulance quickly arrived. I shuffled very slowly, sweat pouring from my brow, to the waiting transport. Morphine, gas and air eased the hurt on the journey. In an NHS Royal Berkshire Hospital bed, they injected more painkillers, before dangling weights from my ankles. God knows why. Mary and Steve visited. Through the haze, I heard Steve say.

"This is not my dad."

Drugged to the eyeballs, I was a wreck in a parallel universe.

In the morning, clothes bundled together, an orderly wheeled me to the private ward, dishevelled, unwashed. Within thirty minutes, undergoing another myelogram I yelled as the pain accelerated. Four hours later, Mr. Theman performed a discectomy to remove the possibility of permanent paralysis.

*A discectomy is a surgical procedure in which the central portion of an intervertebral disc, the nucleus pulposus, which is causing pain by stressing the spinal cord or radiating nerves, is removed.*

*Source: Wikipedia*

Thankfully, the pain subsided, allowing resumption of work on light duties within three weeks.

# Chapter 3
# 1980 - 1999

## Jack's passing

In 1980, Mom and my stepfather moved to Small Heath. They were happy in their new sheltered accommodation. Jack's humour, thoughtfulness and strong character remained until 1984 when he started to suffer from Alzheimer's disease. Over the next five years, we all witnessed the sad wane of a proud handsome man. Mom became his carer, the strain of such responsibility captured superbly in one of her poems.

*I have a sadness in my life, I expect you have one too,*
*There are times when I feel I cannot see the day through.*
*It seems as if I have a burden upon my shoulder,*
*And it just gets heavier as I get older.*
*But I am supposed to be a carer, looking after someone who is ill,*
*So I know I must pull myself together, I can't take a pill.*
*I must not mope, so I pray and hope,*
*That the Lord will grant me the strength to cope.*
*And I know he will listen to my plea,*
*To help me, help the one who really needs me.*
*I try to help myself by writing down all my blessings – and then,*
*I realise how lucky I am and read them over and over again.*
*My thanks to Bert, Vi and Alan for without the support of these three,*
*I just don't know where I would be.*
*Then there is the blessing of a phone call or a friendly letter,*
*They all give me such a lift and make me feel much better.*
*And suddenly I find the world is not all gloom,*
*So I put on some music and dance around the room.*
*I am really going to try, we will have to wait and see,*
*To think more of people far worse than me.*
*Sharing my thoughts has been a treasure that's true,*
*So thank you for letting me read my humble verse to you.*

On 15 October 1989, Jack passed away in East Birmingham Hospital. Heartbroken, my mother wept uncontrollably. When

I consider whether she made the right decision to marry Jack, I think of the occasions they laughed together and tenderly held hands during his illness. Toward the end, soothing his brow as he stared blankly at the wall, Mom turned to Mary.

"I now know why God put me on this earth."

## Ups and Downs

When Norman Deakin moved out of our division, I unsuccessfully applied for the now vacant position...Industrial Tape Divisional Director. An experienced GMM from another part of the company won the right to head up one the business jewels in the 3M crown.

Feedback indicated his extensive marketing experience had been the deciding factor, the Managing Director believing this skill would ensure a more rapid achievement of the commercial objectives than my sales expertise. Consistent with the vast majority appointed to such high-level positions, the new director had also attended university. I was sure this also contributed to the decision, so in order to try and level the playing field, I looked at various distance learning degree courses. I ruminated for six months or so, before Nick, a member of 601 Club, provided the final push.

"All you do is talk about it. I don't think you will ever bother."

The next day, I sought and received sponsorship from 3M to study over a six-year period for an Open University degree.

Whilst disappointed at missing the top job, I had no difficulty accepting such a well-qualified man as my new boss. When planning a reorganisation, he sought input, sharing confidences, before deciding to create Industrial Tape Specialities (an amalgamation of the Industrial and Specialities business). I felt highly satisfied when offered the GMMs position of the largest enterprise in his division and the second largest in the Company.

The first year results of the new conglomerate far exceeded the ambitious targets. I expected to receive the highest appraisal grading available and continue the trend of the previous five years, but in his first formal judgment of my performance, I received a 'B' (exceeded expectations). The explanation that he did not give 'A' ratings seemed irrational and unreasonable. After further discussions, he agreed to change the occasional word, not the grading. The circumstances were not ideal, but I felt strangely reassured when the most senior well-connected GMM in the division confidentially revealed he too had been down-rated and like me had refused to sign the paper work. After a nine-month standoff, with a new appraisal on the horizon, I officially recorded the reasons for not accepting the appraisal and concluded the matter. A month later, the old established GMM confirmed he had accepted his assessment...having convinced the boss to change his evaluation from 'B' to an 'A!' I lost the battle, the old warhorse clearly having a greater influence. Though aggrieved, I kept my counsel. In the ensuing years, the boss never wavered, continuing to say I should be proud to receive a 'B' rating.

## A Bizarre Event

A network of 3M preferred distributor partners, received the lion's share of 'Scotch' adhesive tape orders. In return for our full backing, we asked they decline the option to sell any directly competitive products. In spite of complex issues such as geographical coverage, levels of support and such like, the relationship worked well. Often it seemed they held the upper hand, our bark worse than our bite, but whatever the tensions, both sides undoubtedly benefited from the partnership.

To communicate a new divisional strategic plan, every key distribution principal received an invite to Pennyhill Park, an up market hotel complex in Berkshire. A logistical nightmare, the organising responsibility fell to my excellent PR manager Mike, the master of detail who left nothing to chance. However, even the best plan in the world could never have predicted the illogical bizarre incident on the first evening. Unlike 3M managers, there were no place settings for the two hundred and fifty people guests allowing them the facility to decide on their dining companions. Mike had reserved a seat to my right, in case I needed assistance. Arriving at the table, I recognised eight of the distributors, but not the man sitting in Mike's place, who by his bearing demonstrated he had already consumed a considerable amount of alcohol. He loudly refused when asked politely to find another seat, accusing me of bias against people north of the border (he owned a distributorship in Scotland, so small he should not have been on the invite list). To avoid a major scene, I made a pragmatic decision to allow him to stay. Normality returned for a minute or so. He then looked in my direction, boasting he knew many top 3M executives and could get me sacked. He glared at a guest sitting opposite before enquiring if he was queer (yes, he used that word). It seemed things could not get any worse, but they did.

After another small respite, he stretched in front of me and removed a bread roll from my side plate. I thought he had merely lost his way round the table setting except he then removed with his fork, a roast potato from my dinner plate. I was dumbstruck as were two other guests who had witnessed the incident, their initial amusement turning to bewilderment as he repeated a similar theft from the person to his right. Still drinking, he appeared in a daze, aggressively ignoring constant suggestions he should go to bed. Something had to give. This debacle could not continue. I left the table and spoke to my Scottish regional manager. After another incident, I nodded (the pre-arranged sign, clever or what) and my aide with another colleague, instantly lifted the man from his seat before walking/dragging him out of the room. No doubt taken by surprise, he did not resist. For a few seconds guests remained silent, stunned by the swift conclusion. The rest of the evening went off without a hitch, the extraordinary incident in typical British fashion, becoming the focus of many humorous comments. Hotel reception advised he left at 7am the following morning. I subsequently learned of his alcohol addiction. Why he chose to end an eight-year abstinence at our event remains a mystery. He died six months later.

## Itchy Feet

After five happy years running Industrial Tape Specialities, I started getting itchy feet. The business had achieved substantial sales and profit growth, winning three company awards along the way, but I needed a new challenge. Six months later, the human resource manager advised I was on a very short list to become the managing director of Nigeria.

After sarcastically declining the opportunity, I checked with Mary to see if she harboured any secret desire to live in Africa!

"This is one job you do not have to talk to me about."

Ambition is fine but common sense must prevail. On this day, we both demonstrated oodles of it.

## The Acquisition

Upon being appointed managing director of a European subsidiary my boss left for Europe. An existing board member, a bright engaging personality with a reputation for looking after his staff, replaced him. Canadian Technical Tapes, a major competitor in the European masking tape arena, with excellent manufacturing facilities in Bangor, Northern Ireland, offered quality products at attractive prices, their brand name 'Clipper' well known in the market. Acquiring their European enterprise offered considerable benefits so a detailed study was undertaken.

In the midst of this frantic activity, I continued, in my spare time, to study Social Sciences with the Open University. Concern was expressed that my business effectiveness might suffer because of this academic activity. Having set my heart on obtaining a degree, I ignored the 'drop out' hints, deciding instead to stop claiming course costs from 3M.

In the Bracknell boardroom on a cold December day, five Canadian Technical Tapes executives and a small 3M team, assembled for the formal signing of the legal papers. We were about to make three of their team very rich. Later, everyone involved in the process enjoyed a meal in a Michelin three star restaurant in London. The ex-owner, when not eating, smoked (arrogantly I thought) a massive cigar, celebrating no doubt the additional wealth he had amassed.

It did not come as a surprise when, in addition to my existing assignment, I was asked to assume sales and marketing responsibility for the UK part of this new 3M business. We now had access to a different skill base along with the bonus of a massive new channel to market. Strategically, it made sense to maintain the status quo. Understandably, both distribution channels raised concerns that existing arrangements might change. The politics and nuances needed careful consideration, so from a long worthy list of candidates, I appointed a bright, energetic 3M employee, Tony Stokes, as the sales and marketing manager. He did a fantastic job and after a few other high-level appointments, he moved to St. Paul as a VP.

## A European Appointment

A year after the acquisition, I relinquished all my domestic duties when appointed European Market Manager. Newly created, the role involved the strategic development of the masking tape business across Europe. I now reported to Guy, a director located in Brussels, but continued to work from the UK.

The acquired Bangor plant, produced 'Clipper' and high volume, low profit 'own brand' masking tape. Their focussed manufacturing unit, a major reason for the acquisition, created the opportunity to widen the 3M range. The development of five new 'Scotch' good, better, best constructions, for the industrial, automotive refinish and original equipment manufacturer markets, created significant growth opportunities.

We were now running with the hares and hunting with the hounds, so regular visits to the twelve subsidiaries across Europe became essential. Exchanges were often emotional as many failed to comprehend a 3M strategy which allowed the acquired 'Clipper' and own brands to compete against 'Scotch.' Airports became a second home, dehydration a partner. When I could, I devoted any spare hours to studying the Open University degree modules.

The acquired executive team remained undisturbed but many found big company culture difficult. Their senior director, a charming intelligent person, worked the system well. He knew without him, we might experience problems with his staff and the own brand export business, a market 3M knew nothing about. His observations at the conclusion of the first 3M meeting he attended graphically illustrated the gulf.

"The major difference between then and now is I would hold meetings like this with four staff for half an hour and we would make ten decisions. Today we have twenty-four round this table. We have been here all day and have not made a single decision."

## Degree Obtained

In March 1991, the Open University confirmed I had graduated with a Bachelor of Arts degree. Accompanied by family and selected friends, the uplifting ceremony took place at the Brighton Pavilion in December that year. Immensely proud, it felt a little strange wearing the rented O.U. cap and gown, whilst having lunch in a pub.

At work, my 'bullshit' now had more credibility and colleagues seemed genuinely pleased to have a new graduate amongst their number. Domestically, nothing really changed except I could now proudly hang my photograph alongside my sons and fellow graduates Steve, Simon and Chris.

## The European Dilemma

When Guy retired to France, 3M opportunistically created a Masking and Packaging Systems Division (MPSD) appointing my last UK boss as managing director. High corporate costs continued to be a problem and our competitors, not burdened with such a handicap, used this to their advantage by pricing well below our offer. Consultants suggested a potential solution. The creation of a new company, owned by 3M but operating outside the traditional structure. Even though this radical proposal made absolute sense, the international VP rejected such an out of the box solution. The career-ambitious executive no doubt decided the risk too high in such a conventional company.

The new boss relocated to Italy, close to new 3M packaging plant. Our regular meetings were now held in Milan, the joy of Italian food contrasting with the nightmare of the 'ignore traffic lights' taxi drivers. Surprisingly, twelve months later, 3M announced that our widespread management team of five should be centralised and located in the 3M Europe office in Diegem, near Brussels. With video conferencing and frequent flights making it possible to get together apace, it seemed an illogical costly move.

But the decision had been made. A new transformational policy meant 3M Europe would be my new employer and paymaster, relieving the UK subsidiary of any direct responsibility for my welfare. This significant change meant a Foreign Service employee (FSE) status, normal for a re-location of this kind would not be applicable. The 'package' now on offer, paled into insignificance compared to the generous FSE allowances. In addition, Human Resources assumed that new European staff would either rent or sell their native country living accommodation, removing the need for 3M to subsidise the cost of living in Belgium. Mary and I did not intend to do either so we faced the impossible prospect of running two homes.

From my perspective, I did not see the change in circumstances as a career stepping-stone, unlike a UK colleague, who I am sure, saw it differently. However, he also had problems with the offer. We decided to battle the inadequacies of the re-location deal together, so as a two-person pressure group we highlighted the cost of living difference, entering into numerous conversations with disinterested human resource personnel. After months of wrangling, the senior HR executive, who happened to be from England, entered the fray. He wanted to know why all the fuss, becoming very irritated when he heard the news that Mary and I were not prepared to be out of pocket by any move to Belgium.

"You are setting your sights too high. You should start viewing apartments. They are cheaper."

Blood pressure rising, I barked back.

"If you expect us to move from a comfortable four bedroom detached with a big garden into smaller accommodation with little space, think again. I doubt you would consider giving up your FSE status and move from your rent paid-for abode to a flat!"

Perhaps this struck a chord. Within a week, he rang to advise the deal now included a substantial rent allowance. This significant improvement made a big difference, ensuring at the very least the maintenance of our living standards. Apart from the massive disruption to our life, I now had few reasons to object further. Later, in St. Paul, Minnesota, the collaborating colleague confirmed he had decided to accept the new deal. That evening, recognising the significance of this decision, we consumed, at company expense, a few drams of the most expensive whisky available in the hotel. My negotiating position had now weakened considerably.

I had rejected three prior opportunities to work as an FSE in Brussels. Mary and I had decided we would not consider moving to another country until all the boys had been through or were at university. This intransigence once resulted in a VP visiting us at home, to question our reasoning. He urged we should follow the example of American families who re-locate when and wherever the job takes them.

"Children constantly adapt," he concluded.

With Chris about to finish university we were now in a position to ask pragmatic questions. How would my company react if I again turned down a European position, especially as they had adjusted the package considerably since the start of negotiations? Would the improvement in the pension compensate for living in a foreign country? Would they allow me to continue the role from the UK? In the end, three months after the original offer, the company gave me an ultimatum. To retain my current position, I would have to move to the European headquarters. Not wishing to gamble on the unknown if I remained adamant, we finally made the decision to move.

Although we could have commanded £750 a month to rent Perth Close, we never really considered the option. The thought of somebody we did not know, living in the house, proved a decisive disincentive. When Chris, on finishing university, agreed to move in, it was a mutually convenient arrangement.

Belgium estate agents accompanied Mary and me for forty-eight hours of frantic viewing, avoiding traditional international locations as per our instructions. In line with their reputation, they kept the best until last and one located in a cobblestoned tree lined road, within suited our needs.

Chris moved into Perth Close on finishing university as we re-located in June 1993, to 34, Avenue Belle Vue, Waterloo. This dream dwelling, a short walk from the historic village, had a cellar running its entire length, a vast entrance hall, two separate visitor's quarters, an open plan living room as well as a full expanse of windows leading to thirty-foot balcony. A snip at £1200 a month rent.

3M were paying a large portion of this cost so they participated in the contract process. The property owner to reduce cost, proposed both parties employ one 'expert' to record the condition of the accommodation at the start of our occupancy. This seemed to make sense. After the inspection, the 'expert' sent his findings, written in French. On receiving the English

translation, we completed our own inspection, noting not all chips, scratches and marks had been included in the report. Attempts to get these added were only partially successful as the owner argued we might have created such damage since moving in! A bad omen for the future, as upon leaving, detail in this report would form the basis of assessing any subsequent liability.

We needed to acquire domestic essentials having left the majority of ours in England. I knew departing FSEs left their paid-for furnishings at a warehouse to await auction. Human resources initially reacted coolly to my precedent-breaking request to re-cycle the leftovers, but several days later rather surprisingly they granted permission. After a little persuasion, I purloined a superb hanging chandelier, two bedside lamps, a chair plus two bedroom wardrobes. .

We enjoyed living in Avenue Belle Vue and this provided compensation for an unbelievably stressful job. Together with the rest of the team, I worked ridiculously long hours, often travelling to the twelve countries covered. In 3M's accountancy terms the business was marginal, corporate costs often absorbing any profit. Not pleasant, particularly when most of the loss resulted from elements out of our control. We continually operated on a knife's edge but the boss handled much of the dissension, his upbeat nature and humour playing a major part in maintaining a high morale.

## Corporate Life

Working for a renowned, admired, successful multi-national corporation, was a fantastic but challenging experience. The need for profitable growth to enhance shareholder value ensured the foot was always on the accelerator. Nevertheless having the good fortune to work with great individuals made the overall experience worthwhile. The principle 'be nice to colleagues when you are on the way up, since you might meet them on the way down' ensured relationships between staff at similar levels and across countries continuously developed.

Every twelve months or so, flying Northwest Airlines direct from Heathrow, I would visit company headquarters in St. Paul, Minnesota and no matter what time of year, the weather presented a challenge. In summer, mid 80°F high humidity, massive mosquitoes. In the winter, wind-chill temperatures as low as minus 30°F with an average snowfall of 60-70 inches. Not pleasant.

Over the years, Mary joined me twice (in the summer) enjoying the fantastic hospitality of St. Paul colleagues. When two old stagers visited our shores, we naturally wanted to return their courtesy. With three children in tow, we visited Blenheim Palace, near Oxford, Walt in his old fishing hat, Ed in a posh jacket. They kept firing questions and not wishing to appear ignorant, I blagged the answers. Ed endured until he found it necessary to advise he had graduated in British history. We smiled as he assumed the role of tour guide. On the return car journey, the boys sat on the knees of our guests, singing songs. Mary's unpretentious friendly style, her willingness to embrace the 'family' aspect of corporate life, made her very popular with visitors, especially as she was happy to entertain guests at home.

With instructions to bring swimming trunks, a colleague and I accepted a dinner invitation from a German employee, at his five bedroom 'mansion'. At 9pm after dining, Kurt and his wife asked that we join them at their local club. On arrival, following registration, we both collected a big club bath towel. Kurt led the way dropping my colleague in one area of the changing room, me in another. After donning swimming trunks, I looked around, wondering where to go. Kurt arrived... naked.

"You won't need those," he said.

I felt embarrassed by my embarrassment, since Kurt, standing in all his glory, looked totally at ease. He turned away, pointing his finger as he did so.

"I'll see you in the shower."

O.K. I have been au naturel in showers with men before so what is so different walking around in a private club naked? I felt trapped. I knelt down, putting the trunks into a locker. About to rise, I noticed to my right, the bare, smooth, shapely legs of a naked woman clearly not concerned about my presence. My god, a mixed club. What should I do? Abort or go along with the flow? With no real choice, I tried to hide my abashment by smiling. Shocked, I froze, considering what to do next. Kurt, sensing unease, appeared again, furiously waving me forward. I followed like a lamb to the slaughter, joining the steaming mixed bodies in the shower. I tried not to look around, worried about losing control.

I bashfully ventured into the body of the club, not knowing what to do, particularly with my hands. After walking a few yards, I joined a crowd in a hot tub hoping to see my colleague but he must have been elsewhere. I remained sitting, exposing just the upper body as men and woman moved fearlessly all around me. Eventually, Kurt's naked wife arrived.

"Ope vue are aving a goot time. Vud u like a veer?"

Yes, I know, I know! Sheepishly I walked over to Kurt, already perched comfortably on a barstool, without a stitch of clothing. I had survived so far, but sitting at a bar in the buff was another thing, after all, there has to be a certain amount of decorum! Kurt, in great form, produced a towel asking if we had these sorts of places in England. I tried to look 'cool' stammering a reply. He chortled aloud, congratulating me on staying the course before revealing that my associate had left for the hotel, having declined to participate. So much for 'all for one and one for all.' Gradually I started to relax. After all, I had maintained control and discovered I am not the biggest or the smallest either. Based on limited research...an honourable draw!

Travelling with another colleague, we arrived in Portugal at 9.30pm after a hard day's work in the office to be met by the local managing director dressed up to the nines in sharp trendy clothing. A quiet drink would have sufficed but he drove directly to a nightclub where an attendant greeted him warmly. Already in place, a bottle of spirit dominated the centre of his 'table.' Alluring, stunning, fully clothed women stood around, making it tough not to stare. The M.D. without turning a hair explained, very matter of fact, that we should not attempt any conversation with the girls as it could be interpreted as 'showing an interest' in sex. Probably noticing the beads of sweat on our brows, he suddenly offered re-assurance that the girls had a medical every month, were restricted to one man per night and charged a fixed rate as per government regulations! The comely girls keeping their distance, walked slowly around strutting their stuff. I tried not to catch their eye, but my UK colleague had no such inhibitions. It then took him thirty minutes to shake off her advances.

On the other hand, the girls did not pester our host even though he talked to them. I guess they knew his game. As we left, obviously recognising our discomfort, he casually explained that married men in Spain (and Portugal) routinely attend these type of establishments, to enjoy the ambiance.

"Where else can you enjoy a drink in the company of the most beautiful women in the world, no strings attached, unless you decide otherwise?"

I could not argue with his logic. The rest I can only imagine. After about ninety minutes, he returned 'his' bottle of spirit to a waiter. The following morning, at Company HQ we found him bright and breezy, sitting at his desk. He had dressed down a little. What a trouper.

Compromising beliefs in order to improve the chances of promotion never entered into my thinking. I tried to resist pandering to the hierarchy, refusing to be a corporate politician, instead preferring to give factual, honest opinions, rather than those the bosses wanted to hear. Whilst accepting networking as an important skill in a large organisation, I did not fare well, sometimes failing to get on the wavelength of important people, whereas a UK colleague with years of experience had no such difficulty. He often received a personal invite to sit next to a visiting dignitary and then constantly massaged that person's ego in conversation. I watched in amazement one evening as he shamelessly fawned upon the 3M Chief Executive by congratulating him not on steering company growth but on the fact, he had purchased a ten million dollar house. They then discussed how the Chief Executive would be three hundred thousand dollars better off for every dollar the share price increased. Amazing. Having talent in a corporate environment certainly enabled progress, but nurturing friends on high was the real clincher. The change obtained by this UK colleague to his appraisal rating when I failed, acted as a stark reminder that playing corporate politics was not a strong point of mine!

I often wondered how VPs with global responsibility performed their function. One such executive ruthlessly demonstrated his method. Focus, focus, focus. At the beginning of the year, he would declare his worldwide priorities and concentrate on these, refusing involvement in any other agenda. He would often walk out of meetings without notice, if the subject did not interest him. Rude, yes. Driven, yes. Successful? Very.

Mary and I remained friends with Norman Deakin and his wife after his retirement. He continued to be a passionate outspoken socialist and a strong supporter of Tony Blair. I once sarcastically asked him if, in his eyes, the then prime minister had made any mistakes. He retorted with feeling.

"He has made one. He wore the wrong tie to a dinner party!"

## Unintended Consequences

Late one afternoon our team of six settled in a large office, for a two-hour pre-arranged video conference call with St. Paul. Upon going live at 9.00am their time, we could see the global manufacturing VP together with ten staff, sat around a large table. At our end, the camera focused on two colleagues who also controlled the remote. My manager and I were sitting out of shot. We knew the US technical director was absent, her short, vastly over weight frame hard to miss. Five minutes into the discussions, a loud noise heralded her arrival as she dropped into a pre-assigned seat directly in front of the recording equipment. Settling down, she started to eat a sandwich the microphone picking up every little noise as food entered her ample mouth. My boss shrugged his shoulders as if to say "what the," stifling a laugh. Restraint difficult, we both left the table, burying our heads in the window curtains. Providentially, the two colleagues controlling the video link handled the situation admirably by ensuring U.S. staff could not see our antics. My boss hastily resumed his place at the conference table. I followed seconds later. On sitting down, he mischievously winked.

"Behave yourself."

Embarrassingly, I started giggling again, not regaining composure until the director finished her breakfast. During the break, doughnuts arrived on the U.S. side. I decided not to look!

The expectation was that all subsidiary managing directors would support corporate initiatives. Without their co-operation, the masking programme could not succeed but rightly, they needed strategic logic to allocate resource. On chairing the opening meeting with attendees from each subsidiary, I felt comfortable outlining the plan, English the international 3M language. Nevertheless, by the look on many of the blank faces, it seemed clear the message was not getting across. I assumed they were struggling with the strategy so re-emphasised the major points. A volatile Frenchman, styling himself on Agatha Christie's Hercule Poirot, stood up. Rather impatiently, he said my accent and speed of delivery were making understanding difficult. This bad start did not improve, when in answer to a question, I subsequently produced a written Janet and John explanation entitling the piece, 'fool's guide to manufacturing profit.' A little more thought would have prevented the need to spend the next few months or so building bridges with those European colleagues who had failed to recognise the spirit of the phrase! Happily, this episode did not stand in the way of progress because after much travelling and cajoling, the subsidiaries signed up to the strategy. In the end, I think they even understood my Birmingham accent, which considering I had to grasp all of theirs, was very encouraging!

## Snake Oil

*Wikipedia defines snake oil as 'a derogatory term which if applied metaphorically refers to any product with questionable and/or unverifiable quality or benefit.'*

The career map of an aspiring self-serving USA employee based in the European headquarters, guided him away from mixing with colleagues he judged permanently tarnished with snake oil, eliminating the possibility of his demise by association. I guess, when regularly enjoying our friendliness in the UK he never thought I could be one of those.

An FSE, he managed a profitable developing part of the 3M portfolio. Upon moving to Brussels, he and his wife were kind enough to entertain Mary and me in their home. However, this friendliness was fickle. If he perceived the MPSD business to be struggling he found it tiring to pass the time of day, the change of attitude palpable, but in those periods when we were in profit, he would be his familiar agreeable self. It seemed clear, deciding whether snake oil contamination had started or not, proved problematical for him.

He was resident in Singapore when Mary and I stopped over for a couple of days on our way to Australia. Hearing of our visit, he invited us to dinner. A bottle of wine and a letter of apology, saying he was out of the country for four days greeted us at our hotel. Twenty-four hours later, my camera went missing in the China district, presumably stolen. The police wanted a local contact address so I telephoned his secretary who immediately patched me through to his office. Sheepishly, the 'trainee' VP explained the unexpected cancellation of his trip. He suggested we meet up. It took a second to turn down his kind offer, as I did not want to give him the pleasure of removing his guilt. He did not deserve to be so well treated! Thereafter, I watched his carefully planned career from a distance. His appointment as one of the youngest VPs was expected. His master plan worked, somehow never tainted by his own shortcomings or the failure of colleagues. He indubitably slithered from promotion to promotion!

## Stress the Name of the Game

The notion that working harder could make a difference was part of my thought process. A colleague once arrived at the office at 5am, surprised to find the night watchman awake. As he entered the building, the security man told him of my arrival, thirty minutes before. How stupid.

Every month or so, Mary and I would get together with a work colleague and his wife. We would put the world to rights, inevitably consuming too much alcohol, as we sought to relieve the stress of running a 3M marginal business. We found drowning our sorrows worked, well at least for the evening. Although showing year on year progress, we were finding it tough to achieve a consistent monthly profit, in spite of achieving a 5% price advantage over our competitors. Our masters steadfastly rejected the fixed cost problem, wanting rapid rather than incremental improvement.

On a dark evening, responding to a surprise invitation, an MPSD colleague and I sat down with two directors from St Paul. They had flown from St. Paul specifically to vent their fury at the below forecast European MPSD results. This had apparently caused their international bonus to fall. The bullets fired became personal. They wanted a scapegoat, but we gave as much as we got. The following morning we appraised the boss of the visit. Within a week, he flew to St. Paul, for a showdown with the divisional VP. Whatever happened, it had a positive effect, the incessant inspection thereafter reducing. The visit from the U.S. executives perhaps best illustrates the pressures of corporate life. Relatively happy if expectations are met, oppressive and stressful if results are below plan, even though plausible reasons exist.

## Nissen Solution

For years, random chest pains had stopped me in my tracks. Without any discernible pattern, accurate diagnosis proved difficult, but eventually consultants concluded that neat acid inflaming the oesophagus was the problem. They suggested an operation that involved opening the chest but I declined, opting instead to take a daily Zantac tablet. This solution worked for a short period, but then incidents of the pain returned, but with less intensity. Twice Belgium colleagues rushed me to a local hospital fearing a heart attack, the pill's effectiveness questionable. Benefiting from private health insurance, a local consultant advised a keyhole Nissen operation would solve the problem and eliminate the need for tablets.

*Nissen's fundoplication is a surgical procedure used to treat severe gastro-oesophageal reflux disease (GORD) and hiatus hernia. GORD is the most common disorder that can affect the oesophagus (the pipe that goes from the mouth to the stomach). GORD is where the contents of the stomach, which are acidic, are brought back up into the oesophagus. When this happens, the acid in the stomach causes a burning sensation in the chest (known as heartburn). In most people with GORD, the valve (sphincter) at the join between the oesophagus and stomach doesn't work properly, allowing this reflux of the stomach acid.*

*Nissen's fundoplication involves wrapping the top part of the stomach around the lower part of the oesophagus to tighten the valve. If a hiatus hernia is present (when part of the stomach slides through the diaphragm into the chest), the surgeon will bring the stomach back the original position under the diaphragm. Permanent stitches are used to hold the stomach in place.*

*Source: BUPA*

The operation in a Brussels hospital went without a hitch although the French language spoken by the majority made communication difficult, exposing again my ineptitude at languages. Mind you, when a nurse arrives with shaving cream, razor and towel, little conversation is necessary!

## Defining Moments

Three days after arriving home for fourteen days recuperation, I received a telephone call from a director in St, Paul who after a curt initial health enquiry revealed his true reason for ringing. He demanded a report on his desk within twenty-four hours to

199

explain the month's poor sales results. The insensitivity and lack of compassion surprised and infuriated me. Manifestly, commercial results were more important than the health of an international underling off work after a major operation. Hurt, big time, I rang the office asking the accountant to respond.

For the first time, the possibility of early retirement appealed. Examination of our financial situation revealed we would be able to survive...just. After two weeks, with the future uncertain, I returned to work, determined to carry on as normal but the chest pains soon returned. I expected bad news from the specialist but he confirmed the operation had been successful, acid reflux now impossible because of the newly created value. He concluded logically the original diagnosis was inaccurate and other reasons must exist to explain the continuing pains.

Successful installation of new masking equipment at the Bangor plant finished eighteen months after the acquisition, but problems existed with the re-formulation of tape constructions. At the end of February - two months into a new trading year – with just half the product range available, sales were considerably behind forecast. In a presentation, I gave a visiting executive VP, the accurate assessment that it would be a further three months before every expected construction would be available. Angrily he asked.

"Will the year's forecast be achieved?"

"As we will have lost the ability to trade fully for five months this is unlikely."

Not the answer he wanted to hear.

"Is that a yes or a no?"

What do I say now? There was no way we could make up five months lost sales. Do I continue to tell the truth? My manager answered for me.

"Terry, the answer is yes!"

You can imagine the impact. The VP wanted good news, disinterested in reality. The perception that I was negative would soon become reality, poison in such a progressive company. I tried to forget the episode, ignoring the potential consequences but it had not been my finest hour. When I reflect, I have to ask if my boss was reasonable in interceding the way he did. Giving the VP, the answer he wanted to hear surely did nothing to convince him we would make the forecast so I have to conclude the boss should either have backed me or said nothing, unless of course, a hidden agenda existed.

Six months later, the boss, returned to the UK having taken voluntary retirement. He had managed the smooth integration of Canadian Technical into the 3M organisation, his political nous, intelligence and strong character, steering the ship. I did not agree with all his policies, but under his guidance, sales had grown significantly. Had it not been for the crippling fixed cost factor, the group would have met all profit expectations, a massive achievement.

A new director of Portuguese origin arrived. His appointment surprised everyone. To move from Managing Director of Brazil to a marginal profit group like ours, seemed illogical. The senior executive of an important subsidiary would not aspire to such a position. We later discovered a mini staff rebellion in Brazil, could have contributed to his hurried departure. His distant, aloof approach added little value. The master of delegation, his desk would be completely empty by 10am each morning. The prophetic words of another director came to mind.

"Never go into a group which is losing or has the potential to lose money. Your career will be ruined."

Still suffering severe chest pains, a Brussels doctor felt the problem might be due to work pressure. He recommended it would be in my best interests to move to a less stressful position and offered to write a letter to 3M accordingly. Given the problem had existed for twenty-five years his prognosis was difficult to rationalise. I also worried that the likely solution would be a lower paid, less responsible Brussels based European job. This scenario was certainly not in our interests, but with no let-up in the pain, I reluctantly accepted the medic's advice, submitting his report, with a request to return home to England.

The executive accepted, without argument, the doctor's recommendation. Two months later, the UK managing director, who I had never met, made contact, offering me the chance to work in his corporate marketing department.

I was leaving the European business in a healthy position, the hard yards having created a strong platform for sustainable growth, in spite of all the trials and tribulations. Subsidiaries had accepted the strategy, the two brands co-existed, bespoke trading was strong, the plant in Bangor consistently produced good product. Percentage profit had started to grow. My replacement, a U.S. marketer, had a sound base to take the concern forward.

At our leaving celebration, colleagues presented Mary and me with a specially commissioned watercolour painting of our Avenue Belle Vue house. Such an appropriate gift said everything good about our stay in Belgium.

Today, in profit, the acquisition continues to justify the investment made.

## Living in Brussels

The job in Europe, a mixture of highs and lows, was undoubtedly a most stressful work experience, but the positives of residing in such a delightful country with Mary created an acceptable balance.

Jack and Henny, a sophisticated charming French couple lived next door on our right. We would often converse over the garden fence, Jack encouraging Mary to speak French, whilst requesting her to correct his English. Every four months or so they would organise a classical recital in their superb residence, a glass of complimentary wine finishing the evening in style for the audience of fifty. On the first of May each year, in a wonderful neighbourly gesture, Jack would present Mary with flowers to celebrate d'brin de muguet', a day when Belgium people traditionally give each other a sprig of lily of the valley, to bring good luck.

Our Brussels house with separate visitor's quarters was ideal for entertaining. Overlooking a private garden, the massive cellar provided scope for competitive table tennis or darts. By far our most frequent visitors were best friends, Keith and Alma who on their first car journey took two hours longer than predicted because of my poor directions. Moreover, Simon, Chris, Steve and his ex-wife Andrea experienced a similar problem. There is wonderful video footage of Chris pretending (I trust) to eat the instructions. Obviously, writing route instructions is not a strong point! Thank goodness for GPS. It is impossible to get lost now! The week the family spent in Waterloo was magical...no conflicts, no stress...a loving family enjoying each other's company. We visited all the local sites in the day before relaxing in the evening playing board games, accompanied by a small amount of alcohol! This probably explains why Andrea and I burst into hysterical never-ending laughter when, in a game of Balderdash, the answer 'the cry of a rutting buck' was read out. Yes clearly, it must have been the booze! Throughout the visit, the creative entertainment talents of the family guaranteed a fantastic happy atmosphere. The video camera captured the curtain call on the final night, all the family singing 'Waterloo'. Well it had to be!

Whilst in Belgium, we increased the size of the Perth Close garden fivefold after purchasing land from Waingels Copse School. Integrating the barren tree laden ground into the existing garden needed a skilled approach, so I was most grateful when my brother accepted the challenge. During this period, we asked ourselves an important question. Should savings pay off the mortgage or should we keep the money in the bank at the low interest rates available? Not surprisingly, we decided to achieve a lifelong ambition and own our house outright. Free of the building society felt so liberating.

At 11.30am on Sunday 18 June 1815, in Hougoumont, three miles from Avenue Belle Vue, the Duke of Wellington and Napoleon Bonaparte led their troops into the day-long Battle of Waterloo, where 47,000 troops died. With a 3M colleague and his wife, Mary and I attended the bi-annual re-enactment of the conflict in torrential incessant rain. A massive audience greeted the actors, dressed up to the nines in authentic uniforms. On our left, Napoleon's infantry, shoulder to shoulder in columns, faced Wellington's army across a wide expanse of an open soaking field. Under cover of the chaos caused by charging cavalries, opposing field soldiers advanced on command, firing muskets, engaging in hand to hand fighting. Two incidents spoiled the illusion....the recycling of 'dead' soldiers and the spectacle of a modern ambulance hurriedly weaving its way across the battlefield, blue lamp flashing. In the absence of an announcement rumour abounded. A practical joke, sabotage or was someone actually wounded? The sodden ground made leaving, heavy tiring work. As my mate and I arrived on the safe haven of a footpath, we videoed the girls experiencing problems getting their wellies out of the mud. We watched them struggle, ignoring their cry for help. The girls were not amused, until a gallant smiling Frenchman arrived to escort them across the sludge.

Outside the battleground, participants still dressed as soldiers carrying artificial muskets, carried on with normal day-to-day things...pushing supermarket trolleys, withdrawing cash from an ATM, walking along the street...surreal. The following day, local newspapers reported that 'Napoleon' had actually suffered a minor heart attack. After banishment to hospital, he recovered.

Belgium, a country with bags of culture, history and wonderful restaurants was a most pleasant place to live. At weekends, we would walk into Waterloo village to enjoy coffee, stopping at a crepe restaurant on the way back. The Grand Place Central Square, a world heritage site, easily accessible from Waterloo proved an irresistible draw, so when friends visited, after dinner we would often drive the twenty minutes to enjoy a dessert overlooking the magnificent arena. How debauched! Even though Belgian citizens have a dour reputation, we found them interesting, entrepreneurial, reserved and caring. They were also astute. On three occasions, with colleagues we visited a large residence, where for a fee the owners would serve a superb dinner on their large dining room table, creating a restaurant flavour in domestic surroundings. Not far away from Waterloo, a wine cellar attracted tourists with tasting the norm. The Trappist ale with an alcohol content of 9% contained considerable sediment. Everyone tried it...well, at least once.

It was not easy driving around Belgium. The dreaded *priorite a droit,* where vehicles approaching from the right have precedence, even if coming from a side road onto a main road, unless signs indicate otherwise, proved the biggest challenge. With traffic flow opposite to the UK, the undulating 75km road around Brussels, notorious for its twenty-seven ramps and constant jams, provided little relief. Even in fine weather, adding an extra forty-five minute journey time was prudent when using this infamous road. On a winter evening at 4pm, a mass exodus from the office indicated someone had noticed a snowflake. I did not dawdle, leaving instantly. After an hour or so travelling in slow moving traffic on side roads, I crawled into a row of almost stationery vehicles on 'The Ring'. At the bottom of each sharp gradient, drivers queued whilst cars ahead attempted to ascend the slope. A few made it, but most slid back or stopped. At the third attempt, with wheels skidding furiously I prevailed. After progressing a mere five miles in the next four hours, the traffic suddenly came to a complete halt. I talked to a woman in an adjoining vehicle, cheekily suggesting if stranded, we should cuddle together inside one of our cars for warmth. I interpreted her smile as a positive response. Survival brings out the best in people! After thirty minutes, the traffic started moving again so I never had the opportunity to discover if I had understood her body language correctly. A twenty-five minute journey had taken six hours, 'The Ring' again justifying its reputation as a beast of a road. Mind you, it also provided a link to Bruges the most picturesque of places, Leuven a university town blessed with a fantastic ornate town hall and the Calais ferry. It was on a journey back to Blighty, that I received the last of three mindless speeding tickets. I should have left the Brussels office earlier (stupid) slowed down on the way to work in Bracknell (stupid or what) relaxed on vacation in the Isle of Wight (particularly stupid).

## Leaving Belgium

As the property owner's 'expert' examined the house in minutest detail, it seemed obvious he would find fault when comparing the current condition to his initial report. The game had begun. Our own specialist (at a cost of five thousand

Belgium Francs) was present to ensure fairness, if there is such a thing in these circumstances.

He translated the findings of the opposition.

"There is a little chip on the hob. Three thousand Belgium Francs to repair."

"The slight water drip in the cellar from the overhead pipe indicates a fault. A new valve will cost two thousand Belgium Francs."

"One thousand Belgium Francs to clean the moss off the balcony"

The game was earnest. The goal of the property owner's man to collect more Belgium Francs than his fee, our aim, to keep this amount as low as possible. I took my specialist's advice. Accept the cost of the small items no matter how unjustified, in the hope the filler camouflaging a Wilkins caused hole in the kitchen door and an iron burn in the living room floor (covered by a small carpet square) would go unnoticed. I eventually handed over seven-thousand-five-hundred Belgium francs (£140) to the proprietor's expert, relieved the big cost items had remained undetected. I had matched fire with fire, on balance winning.

We were part of a wider game, well known to all involved. The compensation paid for the identified 'faults' would rarely be used to repair them. The money instead, would go direct into the property owner's account. A new tenant would then receive an initial report acknowledging the damaged items. A profit stratagem for the owner and 'expert'.

## No Place like Home

Chris had moved to a starter home in Lower Earley by the time we moved back into Perth Close. Fencing now surrounded the over grown newly acquired land, but that apart, it was as if we had never left, making repatriation easy. Our normal social life returned and in my new role, I liaised with colleagues to examine the distribution strategic options. Working 8.30am to 5pm stress levels dropped considerably. I found my new boss, the Corporate Communications Director, frustrating though. With no sales or marketing experience, he added little value, but demanded regular unnecessary updates. Risk adverse, he existed in a rarefied atmosphere, success in his world the antithesis of 'does it sell shoes.'

Mary and I started line dancing with Keith and Alma. I thought it would be a doddle. Forward, back, turnaround, that sort of thing. Mary rapidly embraced the art, but my strategy of merely following others did not work. Although tempted to drop out, I decided to learn a few popular sequences in private. Slowly it all began to make sense. We now dressed appropriately. You know cowboy stuff. Mary, patterned blouse, flared skirt, coloured boots. I liked the dark image...black boots, hat, jeans (Johnny Cash like) and patterned shirt. Helen, a traditionalist, transformed our abilities by her methodical patient approach. Occasionally, as part of a small team, we would accept an invitation to demonstrate the art, followed by an hour teaching two simple dances. In vogue, we were in demand. A visit to a rugby club to coach large lumbering individuals, proved an interesting experience. Mary formed part of a lateral row of rugby players, in order to guide them. Similar banks existed to the rear and in front of her. As Helen shouted the moves, total

chaos ensued as the inexperienced tried to sort out their left legs from their right. Amongst all the hilarity, Mary correctly shuffled backwards, hands in the small of her spine, whilst the team's scrum half directly behind, inappropriately moved forward. As they collided, Mary's knuckles pushed against the middle of his slacks. Though it must have been a shock to both of them, they both handled the matter (sorry) with humour and humility. I bet the rugby player had a great buzz relating the story to his mates. I would have done. On two occasions, we joined ten-thousand line-dancing revellers at a holiday camp. Being part of such a large group all moving in one accord to Billy Ray Cyrus singing Achy Breaky Heart is a joy to behold!

Leading a small team of talented colleagues, a 'Recon' at selected 3M distributors over a two-day period involved a staff questionnaire, examination of processes, strategic workshops and analysis of financial data. Having access to company records with an insight into staff dynamics needed a sensitive approach. Betrayal of trust would result in serious consequences, so those participating received a confidentiality agreement and a guarantee that the full report would be restricted to the dealer principal, 3M management receiving an executive summary. Understandably, some refused to allow a key supplier to study their enterprise, but those relaxed with the concept, received free consultancy with a market value of £30,000.

My team knew that distribution staff would be apprehensive, so from the onset we set out to break down barriers with an innovative approach. It proved to be a masterstroke.

"When we arrived this morning you saw four individuals in dark suits, carrying briefcases. As you know, we are a team from 3M, here to help your business. Perhaps not so clear is the fact that we all have interesting claims to fame. Using your observation and deduction skills, we challenge you to say who is who. So here we go. Who went to school with Mick Jagger, who is a line dancer, who drives a traction engine, who is a mountain climber of repute? At dinner this evening all will be revealed."

At this point, the heaviest of our team would pass a sarcastic comment in my direction an indication that banter was encouraged. It worked like a dream, distributor staff joining in the fun as they sought clues, relationships building. At dinner, their own 'claim to fame' often revealed secrets unknown to work colleagues. A dealer principal drove racing cars, a secretary sang in a tribute band and a driver doubled as an Elvis impersonator. At one Recon, a young representative, conspicuously thoughtful, said he had nothing to reveal. To take pressure off, we moved on until he suddenly piped up.

"I do have a claim to fame. I have had sex with xxxxx xxxxx's wife."

A stunned silence followed, given the well-known sporting celebrity mentioned. Sensing the shock, clarification came swiftly.

"At the time we were both single and at university."

Phew, what a revelation. I wanted to ask a few questions but decided discretion is the better part of valour. What can I tell you as a spoiler...nothing really, except the man is a legend in his chosen sport. Interestingly, only eight of the seventy delegates attending the ten Recons, ever succeeded in getting all our claims to fame correct.

We considered replicating the massive Brussels living room in the Perth Close house, by removing the wall of an adjoining room. In the end, we decided to buy at a second hand knock down price, a display conservatory from a local garden centre. With the deconstructed building strewn over the lawn, honest fitters pointed out the problem areas. Later that day, whilst enjoying an afternoon racing at Royal Ascot, a manager from Anglian rang, agreeing without argument to rectify everything.

As expected, we did not make a profit from the racing but we were certainly onto a winner with the conservatory. Erected four weeks later, it has been the best of the many extension investments we have made.

After considerable deliberation brother Keith and his wife Val, proposed a wonderful plan for landscaping the acquired land. We employed Chris, an all-round talented good guy to create the beautifully shaped beds and sweeping paths. On a sunny day, it is an absolute picture.

Student property from the adjoining bicycle sheds has on occasions, found its way into the garden but I doubt whether the most bizarre item found, originated from this source. Whilst walking around the garden on the mobile phone, I looked down at the path. The conversation soon changed.

"Well I have never seen anything like this before. How did they get here? How strange."

"Are you okay?"

"Yes I am flabbergasted. I have found a half set of false teeth lying on the path. "

The colleague on the phone provided an excellent riposte.

"Have you checked they are not yours?"

A stupid question, but I did check, just in case! So how did it happen? Mary thought a magpie might have dropped them when flying past. Mike our next-door neighbour felt they could be the long lost dentures of his deceased mother.

It felt weird to have some stranger's very personal possession in the curtilage of the house so they remained undisturbed. A

few days later, I plucked up enough courage, to give the gnashes a respectful burial in a shallow grave.

For a limited period, 3M UK offered generous voluntary redundancy packages. Knowing my company pension (boosted by our time in Belgium) would sustain a reasonable life style I applied with Mary's blessing. Making such a life-changing decision, thirteen years before the normal retirement age was not easy, but the opportunity seemed too good to miss. No more clocking on or stress from the boss (with the exception of Mary of course) and enough monthly income to enjoy ourselves. The M.D. expressed surprise, but graciously approved the application. After choosing a leaving present, I set a date to leave.

Two weeks later things changed. The M.D. worried about the mass exit of experience from the company, asked me to stay.

His offer of a job grade increase was tempting, but seduced by the freedom retirement would offer, I confirmed my desire to leave. He then changed his tack, asking if I would merely delay departure, to continue the development of the distribution policy. This interesting alternative opened up distinct possibilities of significantly enhancing the pension whilst still having a finite leaving date. After strong, often passionate negotiation, we reached a gentlemen's agreement, nothing in writing. Reporting directly to him, I would delay retirement for two years, in return for an improved remuneration and benefits package.

Working with consultants Arthur Anderson and business managers, the distribution strategy was complete in one and a half years, six months ahead of schedule. Operating within myself during this time, my health improved, tending to confirm the stress diagnosis. However, with rumours the M.D. might be moving on and concerned his successor may not recognise the informal arrangement, I made the 'no brainer' decision...retire. The M.D. kindly hosted a leaving dinner with selected work colleagues and their wives, the original leaving present finally seeing the light of day.

Mary had given me unstinting support all my working life, so as a thank you and to see if we would like a full-blown voyage, I presented her with tickets for a three-day line-dancing cruise from Southampton to Bilbao. A win-win scenario I thought. On the way back, Mary distinctly underwhelmed felt that booking a glorified ferry might not achieve the investigative objective! It would be almost as good as the real thing, I promised.

On 31 July 1997, at the tender age of fifty-four, I retired from 3M after a thirty-year-four-month service.

Leaving the police service, to become a sales representative involved considerable risk. Was it the right decision? On balance, the answer is 'yes.' Although I missed many aspects of upholding the law, working for a fantastic large successful company with great people more than compensated. Did I achieve full potential? It is impossible to tell, but I received adequate reward and retired early on an excellent pension. What more could a man ask for?

*3M 2015.*

*A technology innovator and manufacturer of over 50,000 products. Best known for 'Scotch' tape, 'Post it Notes' Sandpaper and Micropore*

*Worldwide. Employees 89,667. Turnover $30.8 billion.*

*Operations in seventy countries.*

*United Kingdom. Employees 2600. Turnover £516 million.*

## Semi-Retirement

Upon retiring, Mary and I formed M & T Associates (yes, I know, corny) a limited company specialising in strategic planning. For her secretarial work, Mary received a salary, whilst I gave my services free.

Consultancy work occupied no more than two days per week, the pace gentle compared to employment. We started to widen our activities. I had continually hankered after a sports car, so the thrill of driving a newly purchased red MGF, hood down on a sunny Tuesday morning across the Oxford downs to partake in a ceramics course, justified the extravagance. Intending to take more holidays, we joined the Holiday Property Bond (HPB) investing sufficient funds to gain an entitlement of at least two weeks at one of their superb locations.

On the day we left to enjoy the celebration line-dancing cruise, it poured with rain. Parking the car at Southampton docks took an hour due to poor organisation and the varied vehicles accessing the boat confirmed Mary's worst fears…it was a ferry. Soon after departure, the captain advised passengers to purchase seasickness tablets to offset the predicted gale force ten winds. During the twenty-four hours outward journey to Bilbao, through the Bay of Biscay, massive waves battered the ship unmercifully. A distinctive smell invaded the ship as many passengers felt it necessary to use a sick bag. Fortunately, neither Mary nor I required one but trying to line dance proved impossible. In the circumstances, my spouse remained exceedingly tolerant, but under her breath, she must have been cursing that our inaugural 'cruise' had turned into such a disaster. Our return journey did not improve either. The ship departed a mere ninety minutes after arrival, trying to make up for lost time. Unfortunately being flat-bottomed, it could not cut through water like the V shaped hull vessels and continued to sway violently as wind and rain demonstrated their awesome power. On our third sea night with the waves crashing onto the side of the ship with almighty bangs, Mary finally expressed genuine concern.

"I don't think this boat is able to take much more."

I put on a brave face, in spite of sharing her concern.

"Everything will be alright darling."

It is worth pausing here for a second, as this exchange of words summarises neatly a difference in our personalities. Mary is consistently more likely to take a pessimistic view of situations, than I am. They say opposites make a match and in our case, this is true.

Anyway, I digress. The gale continued and we tried to make the best of a bad job. I visited the packed bar, two hours from Blighty, surprised by how many passengers were enjoying themselves. I started to spout about the weather, cursing we were eight hours late. A man, leaning heavily on the bar disagreed. According to him, it had been a great trip given the continuous availability of duty free drink. Others around him agreed!

We reached Southampton at 1.30am to find the main car park locked. The complaining key holder finally arrived and we departed at 3am, for a sixty-minute drive to Reading, the ordeal finally over.

The trip could not have been worse but at least it confirmed one thing...we did not suffer from seasickness - a big bonus.

## Mom Down South

After Jack's death, Mom continued to live in the sheltered accommodation in Small Heath, near friends and relatives. We tried to visit every month. Not the best of geographical locations, she nicknamed the area, 'Bangladesh'! Horribly, within a single year, at the tender age of eighty-five she had to confront a masked robber in her living room and suffered two muggings. Frightened to be on her own or go outdoors in a decaying area, we suggested she relocate down south.

In late 1997, she moved into Perth Close. We converted the games room into a private living space. With plenty of light, it had all the necessary comforts...a television, a chair, a settee. We wanted Mom to continue to have her own space, but be part of the family. After a short period, it became clear not all was well. She stopped writing her beloved poems and began crying without reason. Worryingly, her healthy appetite disappeared. Diagnosed with depression, bought on by recent traumas, she started taking doctor prescribed tablets. Although things improved, we grew concerned about our ability to cope in the future. Tensions grew. We were not caring for an Alzheimer's patient, but we were ill prepared to deal with the emotional roller coaster.

Then, after twelve months, a ministering angel appeared.

We sought advice from social services, receiving a subsequent visit. The seraph listened intently before advocating that Mom should move into local sheltered accommodation to regain her independence. Although reacting negatively at first to this surprise suggestion, after further discussion mother agreed to consider the option.

We travelled in silence to James Butcher owned housing in Dyers Court. Mom's thunderous face conveyed her unhappiness. By suggesting another move, she probably felt we were pushing her out, confused and frightened at the uncertainty. Then she met Steph the manager, welcoming, friendly and humorous. Mindful of an old person's potential thoughts she brilliantly sold the benefits of living in sheltered accommodation. On our way out, we bumped into Betty, a shy retiring resident!

"If you are considering moving in, you'll need a good sense of humour. Last night we held an Ann Summers party to make sure we remain sexy even at eighty!"

Mom laughed, visibly relaxing by the minute. As we left the building, she glanced back smiling. A few weeks later, she moved into Dyers Court, situated near the Woodley shopping centre and just three minutes away from Perth Close.

With her own front door, the apartment featured a living/kitchen room, separate bedroom, bath and toilet. She calmly settled into her new way of life, joining in the organised activities, her warm engaging nature winning many friends. She began writing verses again (a sure sign normality had returned) and needed a 'secretary' to type her work. After an interview, I secured the job.

"You are cheap," her joyful explanation.

She could take weeks to compile a rhyme. She would scribble initial thoughts on bits of paper, think about the subject, reconsider, add, subtract, before finishing the piece. Nothing escaped her active fertile mind and she could seamlessly move from the funny to the poignant. Her poems were invariably well received, the thoroughness, attention to detail and no nonsense approach making them very easy to read. I am sure this insect would have been flattered.

> *I was having an extremely restless night,*
> *And I had a strange feeling that things weren't quite right.*
> *Although the night was warm, I felt cold to the bone,*
> *There was this feeling, I was not alone.*
> *As I switched on the bedroom light, my eyes grew wider,*
> *For lying on my bed, was a whopping great spider.*
> *What to do? Should I ring the bell, raise an alarm,*
> *But perhaps the intruder meant me no harm.*
> *Up and down the bed he crazily ran,*
> *Enjoying a game of 'catch me if you can'.*
> *At two in the morning I am not feeling my best,*
> *And could have killed this spider, for disturbing my rest.*
> *But I caught him in my hanky, quite tenderly, not rough,*
> *I didn't want to hurt him, but I had had enough.*
> *Before he was released, to this spider I had something to say,*
> *"If we have to keep meeting, could we make it in the day?"*
> *"For aren't you the spider I met on the garden path,*
> *And didn't I find you in my bathroom, using my bath?"*
> *Now spiders are alright in their place,*
> *But I don't want them squatting on my pillowcase.*

*So Mr. Spider let me make one thing clear,*
*Please, keep away from me, I don't want you near.*
*And if ever I want someone to share my bed,*
*I've got Roger the Rabbit or Long Legged Ted.*

She never stopped communicating this way, her words engendering heartfelt emotion and happiness in equal measure, to people of all ages. She would even accept unpaid 'commissions.' I often benefited from her ability to consume facts and turn them into a rhyme. Due to propose a toast the lassies on Burn's night, I asked Mom if she would write about The Bard. She knew nothing about the man so researched the subject. I proudly read out her work on the evening.

*Robbie was born in Ayrshire, under a lucky star without a doubt,*
*His folk were poor and plain folk and that is what he wrote about.*
*Robbie loved women and with them he spent many nights,*
*But he also respected them and fought for their rights.*
*Mind you Robbie was quite a laddie,*
*For twelve times he became a daddy.*
*But in between the patter of little feet,*
*He wrote endless verses and songs so sweet.*
*His talent was so great and versatile that,*
*He could write a verse at the drop of a hat.*
*Robbie's legacy is there for all of us to enjoy,*
*Whatever race, creed, whether girl or boy.*
*There will never be a New Year without 'Auld Lang Syne'*
*It fills our heart with cheers and tears…it is without time.*
*And although Robbie died prematurely at thirty seven,*
*He is now no doubt looking down on us from heaven.*
*Oh Robbie you were so clever,*
*Your lovely songs and poems will stay with us forever.*
*That is why there will always be a Burns Night,*
*For Robbie you are clearly Scotland's brightest light.*

## Father Dies

In 1997, Dad moved from Berkeley Road into a nearby care home, suffering from early stages of dementia. Edie visited every day, whilst Mary and I travelled from Reading as often as possible. I hated the place. The smell of stale bodies. People waiting to die. Surrounded by less capable inmates, his mind soon deteriorated. During our last visit, he quietly rubbed his fingers over our family photographs, smiling affectionately. He died shortly after, on 11 August 1998, aged eighty-eight. After the funeral service, surprised at my emotion given our disjointed relationship, I moved away from the crowd into the Garden of Remembrance. Thoughtfully, Steve, sensing discomfort, joined me.

"What are you thinking?"

Tearfully I replied.

 "He was my Dad."

For the next five minutes or so, in solitude, I thought about him.

Born in Yardley, Birmingham, 29 December 1910, educated at local secondary school, he excelled at football, playing on the wing in a very successful team, many of whom progressed to the paid ranks. A handsome, slight, gentle, polite, modest man he asked for little, comfortable in his own skin. He rented accommodation in Berkeley Road, Hay Mills (the place of my birth) and lived there all his adult life (except for his last year) during which time he worked as a forklift driver for just one company, not interested in developing his undoubted artisan talents. He never passed his driving test relying instead on two lifelong mates to ferry him around. A marvellous ballroom dancer he also graced the snooker table, captaining two local teams. Although he once beat Graham Miles, later to play in the professional world final, he rarely spoke of this achievement. Strongly left handed and a heavy smoker he volunteered for the Home Guard during the war, not being eligible for conscription. In my sorrow, I felt angry that a marriage split, so frowned on in those days, had created a situation where we really did not know each other.

Edie continued to live alone in Berkeley Road. Mary and I decorated the living room, tarnished by heavy nicotine stains, as best we could. Cleaning the wallpaper encouraged years of cigarette tar to rise to the surface, five coats of emulsion barely covering the stain. She coped reasonably well, facing the loneliness maturely, but two years later moved into an old people's home on the Chester Road, Aldridge. After six months, she stopped eating, dying peacefully in her sleep. Edie deeply loved my father for over twenty-five years providing him with the real happiness he clearly did not enjoy with my mother. I respected her.

In February 2009, unexpectedly, a letter from Prudential arrived suggesting I should ring a specific office. After answering searching questions, the employee proudly announced he had at last found the person listed on a policy. Two weeks later, I received a £1750 cheque, the value of the life assurance Dad had taken out on my life. A poignant occasion, it proved, even though I did not see him often, he had not forgotten me.

What do I make of it all? Well, whatever the reasons for the separation, they were grievous. My brother and I did not benefit from having both parents around, rare in those days, yet our upbringing could not be described as traumatic. It would be naïve however to say it did not have an emotional consequence. In spite of a confident exterior, re-assurance of feelings is important to me. I have never taken Mary's love for granted, forever hoping to hear her say, "I love you." Perhaps this is normal, but I surmise my need is more fundamental than most.

## Retirement

In August 1999, after two years providing consultancy services to six concerns, Mary and I decided to wind up the company. It had been a profitable enterprise but the time felt right to retire completely.

We started to do everything and go everywhere together unhindered by bosses or commitments, but three months after full retirement, our new life needed a little adjustment.

"Isn't retirement great? We have settled into it so easily!" I said assuming Mary would heartily agree.

"It's alright I'm enjoying it, but there is a small problem. You think your life has changed a lot. Imagine the difference in mine. I have no space at all now."

Frankly, I had never considered this aspect. Together 24/7 represented a massive sea change especially for Mary, comfortable spending hours on her own. Things had to change so I decided to take up golf again.

## Police Support Volunteers

It had always been my intention, to offer my gift of time to a good cause. I wanted the experience to be progressive, varied and contribute to something or someone, but had no pre-conceived ideas. A discussion with the local neighbourhood watch leader led me to Thames Valley Police (TVP). They were looking for volunteers to provide occasionally, their gift of time, not as warranted special constables, but as civilians without powers. Two months later with seventy other applicants, I attended a Police Support Volunteer (PSV) induction evening in Reading. A seemingly disinterested ageing superintendent accompanied by a sprightly inspector explained the concept, the benefits to TVP but ignored what it would mean to the individual. At the end of a poorly constructed event, the inspector over coffee honestly explained that the volunteer plan had no real framework. It appeared a 'good idea' concept had been unveiled with scant thought of how to turn it into reality. Before departing, I suggested my skill set could benefit the programme. For nine months, I heard nothing, not even a letter.

Concluding they did not want my voluntary services, I wrote a letter of resignation. Mary's suggestion that it was more of a 'come and get me' plea, proved correct. Two days later, the inspector rang. I agreed to help him with the project. In accepting the role as the PSV coordinator for the Berkshire West Business Command Unit (BCU), I knew the challenge would not be easy given a culture wary of difficult to measure initiatives.

The PSV concept offered a new type of volunteer support but the well-intentioned scheme was in disarray. Communication had been poor. Staff and unions were reticent, concerned that jobs could be affected. Many volunteers felt unappreciated whilst others were just ignored.

Only urgent action would give the enterprise any chance of survival. The development of a short snappy strategic plan emphasised three action strands. Reduce scepticism, develop suitable roles and processes, create an organisational framework to move forward. At a quarterly meeting, the umbrella theme 'use them or lose them' jolted the executive into action. The area commander, not wishing to look a gift horse in the mouth, immediately directed his staff to examine the opportunities. He agreed to champion the programme. This immediately changed the atmosphere. Within a few months, most volunteers were heartily engaged in meaningful tasks. Gathering pace, hitherto insurmountable barriers suddenly disappeared, a sign that even in a fiercely protective culture, logic and commitment can drive change. I created a volunteer management team, organised regular social functions communicating successes. Over time, PSVs became an accepted part of the furniture, helping in tasks such as admin, front counter, witness sitting and CCTV monitoring.

With one hundred and twenty PSVs, the Berkshire West model quickly spread to other departments. Having completed the task, unable to add any more value I resigned soon after appointing my successor. The area commander acknowledged my contribution with a commendation.

*'Mr Terry Wilkins is commended for his generosity in giving up his time to lead the Reading with Wokingham Police Support Team and for his undoubted enthusiasm and professionalism that has formed this group into a durable and essential part of our policing strategy without which our service to the public would suffer.'*

A short time later, following the appointment of a full time manager to lead the TVP programme I accepted an approach to return to the fold as a volunteer and abet Mary B, the new Oxford based boss.

We soon developed an overarching strategic plan. This included a volunteer investment audit (VIVA), which proved that for every £1 TVP invested in the PSV programme they would receive a return of £2.90. As a result, the Police Authority agreed to finance a coordinator in each of the six BCUs. This major commitment established an important principle...PSVs were now part of the policing plan.

Whilst staff apprehension reduced, local Unison representatives maintained the pressure by voicing their concern over the increasing numbers. Mary B and I acted as a team, addressing issues as we went along to make sure problems did not fester.

# Chapter 4

# 2000 - Present

## Chris in New Zealand.

A young Chris was able to use charm to achieve his aims. Never shy, he would chat to anyone who would listen and won a talent contest at Pontins, as a stand-up comic. Whilst at school, he appeared in several plays receiving rave reviews, the most notable for his performance as a pantomime dame. His love for fishing started at a very early age and developed to the point where he would spend all night trying to pull elusive carp from local lakes. He worked at 'Just Tiles' during the weekends and enjoyed composing and playing his own music, a hobby he has continued ever since.

After graduating from Crewe and Alsager College (now Manchester Metropolitan University), he returned to Reading, living in Perth Close whilst we were in Brussels. He broadened his work experience and married for the first time, but it did not work out.

He then met Lindsey and moved permanently to New Zealand in 2000, for the birth in Wellington, of his lovely daughter Ruby Mae on 18 May. The 'windy city' on the North Island is a great place for coffee bars, atmosphere, food, distinctive harbour and friendly people.

Ruby now lives with her mother in Paraparaumu, thirty miles from Wellington and is a loving, confident young person, who fills a room with her winning sparkling personality. Her other grandfather Ken Griffiths, lives nearby, in a magnificent dwelling, but since 2012 has been alone, following the sad, premature death of Ruby's brave lovely grandmother Barbara.

Mary and I have spent many a happy hour with Ken and Barbara in the 'Elvis Presley' games room enjoying the most marvellous hospitality, Ken's exquisitely cooked breakfasts helping to overcome any hangovers. We remember Barbara with the utmost affection.

Chris embraced the Kiwi lifestyle with aplomb, becoming a fan of the Wellington Phoenix football team and the All Blacks. He met Jacqui after an unsuccessful second marriage and now works and lives happily in Nelson on the South Island with Jacqui and her daughter Mae. On the 31 May 2014, he became a father again, to beautiful Imogen Mary who I am sure will become an expert at playing the Japanese drums one day, just like her mother.

If playing the Recon, 'Claim to fame' game, Chris would probably choose these, from many on his list.

His appearance with Bob Monkhouse in TV show 'Wipeout' reaching the final.

The time he won £10,000 as a contestant on 'Catchphrase' (with Roy Walker as compere).

## Mom on the Move Again

Steph maintained an active social calendar at Dyers Court making it a happy place. Close friendships developed, residents looking out for each other. The day they heard the building was to be demolished due to asbestos problems, must have been a crushing blow to the elderly residents. It troubled mother.

*I have a dream; I know that's it a silly dream,*
*But oh, if only it was part of Butcher's scheme.*
*And if only my reverie would become real,*
*How much happier, we in Dyers would feel.*
*If we knew we were going, where we wouldn't be parted,*
*And things would be the same as when we started.*
*We have been happy in Dyers Court with what we had,*
*The thought of leaving it all makes us feel so sad.*
*Like any large family, we have got used to one another,*
*We would help out with little things, never any bother.*
*Now all of a sudden our lives will be changed,*
*Somewhere else to live, so much to arrange.*
*In Dyers Court we felt cared for and protected,*
*Now we are feeling like parcels, waiting to be collected.*
*I love my little flat, I love every door,*
*Now I'm having to leave, I love it twice as much as before.*
*Writing this down, won't do any good I know,*
*But I have to show, that it is really hurting so.*
*We will get through it and it will be nice when we come back,*
*But just at the moment things are looking black.*
*I sound as if I am in the depths of despair,*
*I just wish that we weren't going anywhere.*
*But staying on familiar ground,*
*With people we know and love all around.*
*Like matured plants, we didn't want to be uprooted,*
*In Dyers Court we were blossoming, in soil that suited.*
*Butchers tell us not to worry, that's easier said than done,*
*For what is about to happen, won't be a barrel of fun.*
*The mind boggles, at what a task it will be,*
*Will it keep us happy? We will just have to wait and see.*

Three alternative residences, all within five miles were proposed. At the start, Mom declined to commit but eventually, two years after moving into Dyers Court, she re-located to Catherine Court four hundred yards away, worried about the loss of friends who had chosen differently. However, her adaptability soon came to the fore and inspired by the building manager Oscar, she soon settled.

## What Age?

Mom was born 12 August 1914. Birthday celebrations were usually quiet affairs. She particularly appreciated cards with eloquent expressive sentiments, no doubt reflecting her own wordsmith ability. We marvelled that her mental agility showed no sign of deteriorating, even as a nonagenarian. On the other hand, she down-played her age, having no desire to discuss the time she would receive congratulations from the

Queen, even though we constantly reminded her that 2014 was not far away.

We learned the official records at the Department of Pensions and those of her doctor showed a different year of birth than we thought, so I contacted the General Register Office (GRO) requesting a copy of her birth certificate. The helpful registrar asked me to hold whilst he searched the archives. A few minutes later, he advised he could find no trace of the said Eileen Ridgers, born 1914.

"Try 12 August 1913," I suggested, a date on one of the official documents.

I again received a negative answer.

At this point, my mother did not officially exist. The registrar, sensing my surprise and bewilderment kindly agreed to delve further. I waited, wondering what would happen next. After thirty seconds or so, he announced triumphantly he had found Eileen Ridgers, nee Hall, born 12 August 1912 in Birmingham. It made no sense. Mom had repeatedly said she was born in 1914. Did she have a mental block? Why the pretence? Why the variation on official documents? When I telephoned, she abruptly slammed the phone down on hearing the news. An hour later, she tearfully confessed to living a lie. When aged fifty-two, she apparently applied for a job not available to those over fifty, so in consequence knocked two years off her age. Having obtained employment she found it necessary to carry on the lie...and had never corrected the misinformation since then! Amazingly, this deception had finished up on official papers. This raises the intriguing possibility she did not claim her old age pension until sixty-seven, that at seventy-two she celebrated her seventieth birthday and so on. It may also explain why she hated talking of her age. We subsequently discovered other errors on official documents. Her marriage certificate (to Jack) shows her age as fifty-six when she was in fact fifty-seven. The provider of a small pension recorded her date of birth as 1914. It makes you wonder how it was possible for so many formal documents to record incorrect, different dates of birth...I guess no real double-checking and Mom's persuasive manner in her determination to hide the truth.

Embarrassment over, she then embraced her true age, loving it when the family created a celebrity approach by clapping as they do on TV, when making an imaginary announcement.

"Welcome Eileen Ridgers aged (let's say) ninety-three."

She would join in the fun; hold her arms aloft to milk the acclaim, free at last from the lie.

Two years or so after Mom moved into Catherine Court, an announcement the building would have to be demolished, again surprised residents. On this occasion though, apart from the disruption, the news had a positive aspect...they would henceforth live in new purpose built accommodation in the grounds once occupied by Dyers Court. This fourth move in six years must have been highly stressful but she took it all in her stride, contented most of her new and old friends would be similarly located. The owners, wonderfully sympathetic to her deteriorating eyesight and increasing frailty, allocated her a superb two-bedroom apartment with all the amenities, near a lift on the first floor. The move to 'The Chestnuts' went smoothly but Mom was disappointed that Oscar did not secure a position. Typically, though, this did not stop her welcoming the new manager.

*Welcome Christine we are glad you are here,*
*The welcome is a little late but none the less sincere.*
*You walked into our lives Christine, no ceremony, no fuss,*
*No welcoming party for you, there was just us.*
*There you were, cool, calm and collected,*
*We didn't know what we expected.*
*But we found you smiling and nice,*
*It didn't take long to cut through the ice.*
*We knew that you would help us when you could,*
*Along with your lovely sense of humour, it had to be good.*
*We know you have been taking it at your own pace,*
*For putting a name to each face.*
*Quite a daunting task without a doubt,*
*But it didn't take you long to sort us out.*
*We want you to be happy here Christine in every way,*
*Because we like you and we want you to stay.*

Mom soon became part of the furniture, popular as ever. We did have a few dramas though. On three occasions in a month, Guildford central control telephoned in the middle of the night to advise she had pulled the emergency cord suffering from shortage of breath. Each time I found her chatting cheerfully to the paramedics, panic over. They expressed the opinion that Mom was lonely, so after providing re-assurance that we would never fail her, she did not needlessly call them out again.

Once she had settled, Mary and I felt more confident to take a vacation, convinced the James Butcher organisation and friends would care for her. Nonetheless, she tended to become agitated when we were due to go away. Fearing we might upset her more, we made a conscious decision to avoid phoning whilst on holiday. On a visit to South Africa with Keith and Alma, Steve rang to advise his grandmother was in hospital suffering shortage of breath. This had happened before, invariably resulting in a quick resolution, the problem analogous to the paramedic incidents. An early discharge did not occur, but at the back of our minds, we harboured the niggling thought that Mom was again making the most of her ills. This all changed following Steve's next communication and I prepared to return home, the problem appearing grave. Then surprisingly, we learned of her discharge, much to everyone's relief. We again decided not to telephone, fearing she might fret more on hearing our voice. After the holiday, Steve diplomatically raised

the subject. He said we should always ring Mom when away...we were after all the two people in the world she cared about the most. When put in such a way, it seemed so logical and of course, thereafter we always made contact.

Although Mom had been writing poems all her life, very few were on file. She lost most of them to well-meaning friends who had promised to find a publisher. Part of my personally written job description as her honorary unpaid secretary was to edit, type and safely store her current work. In 2005, she sobbed emotionally when presented with 'Verses of My Life' a hard book compilation of the poems I had on file. A legacy for the family and to make Mom happy had been the only objectives, but on a whim, I rang the local BBC office. Twenty-four hours later she appeared on the BBC South programme to help the station celebrate the officially designated Poet's Day. An immaculately conceived plan? No pure luck.

She giggled excitedly on hearing the exciting news and agreed not to tell anyone (in case of a hitch). Thirty minutes before the TV reporter was due, I arrived at her flat. She held up her favourite multi-coloured dress.

"Is this OK?"

"You will look fabulous. You've not told anyone have you?"

"No, you told me not too."

Her helper in the kitchen let the cat out of the bag.

"Great news about your Mom appearing on TV."

The doorbell rang at 11am prompt. Alan Sinclair a reporter from BBC South had arrived. No back up crew. An interviewer, video man and editor all in one.

"That is the way it's done nowadays," he advised.

She performed perfectly. A two take wrap. Alan left after forty-five minutes. An hour later the BBC lunchtime show, featured Mom reading a poem, to advertise the evening slot. At 6.30pm, BBC South Today presented the full piece. It is now on 'You Tube,' titled Eileen Ridgers, Poet.

Subsequently several newspapers ran the story and the book found its way into the Reading and Woodley libraries. The local Age Concern purchased twenty-four copies. Occupants at 'The Chestnuts' embraced her celebrity. She loved the attention and donated the cash generated, over £1000, to an Alzheimer's charity in memory of Jack.

I casually remarked that it would be possible to publish a second edition if she could write another hundred poems. Said with tongue in cheek to keep her mind active, I did not really expect her to rise to the challenge but in spite of deteriorating health, she continued to put pen to paper. As the verses piled up, she would often say her friends wanted to know if there were enough for another publication...a canny approach to get answers to her own question! I really lacked the motivation, but hoist by my own petard, I started to compile a file of her new unpublished work.

After a fall, Mom became an in-patient at the NHS Trust in Wokingham. Banished to a side room, she hated the isolation, unable to talk to other patients. It came as a massive surprise to learn she had MRSA. Mom was blissfully unaware. With the stigma attached to this bacteria, we became concerned at the reaction of her friends should they find out. James Butcher medical staff and our local doctor provided some comfort when they confirmed her bacterial infection was too small to be contagious so would remain confidential. Discharged after four weeks she returned to 'The Chestnuts' none the wiser.

## Simon in Australia

When old enough, Simon started earning extra pocket money working at a radio and TV shop at the weekends. He did not shirk, confronting the 'house rules' and my rigid attitude. Mary. We had a few battles along the way but, eventually, as always, compromises were agreed. A talented actor he secured, whilst at school, the main role in Charlie and the Chocolate Factory and Romeo and Juliet. Following an audition, he obtained the lead part in a 30-minute TV play called 'The Winner' and later joined The National Youth Theatre. It seemed he would follow a thespian career after graduating from the University of Bristol, but it was not to be. He backpacked around the world, twice returning to Australia on work sponsorship visas, clearly favouring the superb beaches and lifestyle. He fell in love with Melina, bringing his future wife, to live with Mary and me in 2003, the year before they married at the magnificent Stoke Park, Stoke Poges, the location famous for the films Goldfinger and Bridget Jones Diary.

The inevitable happened early in 2004, when Simon left these shores permanently, to live with Mel in her homeland. It was an emotional departure, as for a second time, another son moved to the other side of the world to join a seventy strong Italian family, the Leonellos, such superb generous warm folk.

Mel and Simon have two, bright, engaging children: Josh born in 2007 and Kiana in 2009. Although they have recently separated, Simon and Mel are firm friends and are devoted to their kids. Whilst he moves to another chapter in his life, Simon continues to follow his career in publishing, where he has spent most of his working life.

Simon's friends in Australia may not know:

He knew Simon Pegg at University

One of his mates is the successful musician Andy Price, responsible for writing the Robin Hood TV theme.

## Additional Volunteer Responsibility

When Mary B decided to travel the world, she asked if I would be her temporary replacement. I hesitated to return to paid work, but emotionally involved, agreed to work three days per week over six months, so she could fulfil her dream. I signed with Reed Employment Agency, the constabulary route for temporary employees. Rarely experiencing a high-rate taxpayer accepting a poorly paid part-time job, their systems could not deduct more than the standard rate of tax. After a tortuous process, a bright helpful woman sorted it all out. She proved to be the daughter of a 3M colleague. What a small world!

Working from 7.45am until 3pm at TVP's Kidlington headquarters, amongst staff I knew, created few problems, though the atmosphere could have been better. A permanent sterile atmosphere existed. No chatter or humour, merely stern faces. Designated the 'gold command room' the continuous streaming of news via a bank of wall-mounted televisions, appeared to stifle any conversation.

Thankfully, Julie, a highly intelligent friendly new employee, made the one-hour travel each way worthwhile. She provided terrific support. The number of PSVs within TVP had now risen to three hundred and seventy five and Unison, the employee trade union, expressed concern that because of the rapid growth it was likely some of the roles performed could undermine staff functions. This challenged the fundamental of the programme...volunteers do not replace staff but provide 'additionality'. After examining the policies and inspection processes, the Unison rep accepted the suggestion to visit unannounced, locations where PSVs were providing support, a bit like a mystery shopper. At a subsequent meeting, he expressed satisfaction at the scheme's integrity, meaning we could continue to grow with minimum interference. Shortly afterward, the Unison office accepted administrative help from a PSV. This has continued ever since.

Six months after holding the fort, I resumed my normal volunteer duties. In late 2004, the Association of Chief Police Officers (ACPO) appointed Deputy Chief Constable Chris Lee, Dorset Police, as the national PSV portfolio leader. After helping him prepare the terms of reference (TOR) for the new national PSV programme board he asked if I would become, on a voluntary basis, his national manager. I readily accepted, with the proviso I would also stay with TVP.

The public are the police and the police are the public is a well-known 'Peelian' principle, as true today as in 1829 when Robert Peel, the Home Secretary established the Metropolitan Police. This notion underpins the idea that communities should decide how they wish to be policed and in doing so become more responsible for their own destinies. The nature of the concept acknowledges that community volunteers from any walk can break down barriers and help to make their environment safer. Thus, from a PSV perspective, the perfect organisational model would ensure full inclusivity, involve all cultures and be representative of the society served.

A survey revealed there were three thousand eight hundred PSVs nationally, but many of the forty-three constabularies were totally ignoring the benefits of implementing such a programme. Immediate priorities appeared clear...prove the benefit strategically, spread good practice, raise the PSV profile, communicate newly developed tasks and bring energy to the table. The National Police Improvement Agency (NPIA) was supposed to help with the co-ordination of national activity, but gaining their active involvement was like trying to get blood out of a stone. In order to move things forward I needed the essential assistance of police staff throughout the country.

The inaugural PSV national conference held in February 2006 at the Hilton Hotel in Gatwick, attracted over a hundred delegates from 80% of the forces in England and Wales. Co-operation across the service improved with local emphasis established through a working party. In 2008 the assignment of a new team to the policy unit at NPIA, transformed the relationship. Within their web site, the creation of a PSV

section facilitated a knowledge base. All these things combined, to provide much needed focus.

In November 2008, the Association of Chief Police Officers acknowledged my

efforts with a presidential award. Sara Thornton, the then Chief Constable of Thames Valley Police made the presentation.

The citation read:

*'In recognition of his tireless enthusiasm, determination and in respect of developing the concept of Police Service Volunteers (PSV) nationally, his lead role for the national working group and as project coordinator and member of the PSV Programme Board. During this time he was instrumental in planning the first national PSV conference and currently manages a number of work streams that continue the development of PSVs. His knowledge, contribution and dedication has informed the direction of this work and for this Mr. Wilkins is commended.'*

 A national 2009 – 2013 PSV plan provided focus and featured a memorable logo developed by my brother Keith. Released at the second national conference, it raised the profile and credibility of the scheme.

The assistance provided by PSVs is often unglamorous and mundane. The expanse of tasks performed are too numerous to mention, so if we take extremes it should provide a perspective. They range from puppy socialising to administration, from crime prevention to research, from customer reassurance to mentoring. Several constabularies have been slow in embracing the idea and whilst this is disappointing, it is perhaps understandable, given the differing nature of requirements across the country and the autonomy each force has in decision-making. Nationally, staff associations and unions continue their opposition, failing so far to embrace the fact that a helping hand is not a threat and can make a big difference to over-stretched employees.

Managing a third sector organisation takes certain skills. There needs to be an understanding of the ethic, the nuances involved and a big dollop of common sense. This is why experience is vital. To ignore the fact that a volunteer needs managing differently from staff is a recipe for disaster. Citizens giving their time freely ask for little in return other than feeling a valued part of the surroundings. However, in reality it is not as simple as that. Volunteers can be unpredictable, demanding, pains in the butt, wonderful, generous, and inspiring. All of these and more.

The case of the ex-army officer, who took on the very authority of TVP, almost winning, stands out. His task, to help two mornings a week on the front counter of a semi-rural station, changed when the paid employee went off long term sick. He then turned up five mornings a week becoming part of the furniture. Force policy prohibited volunteers wearing a uniform yet the local inspector allowed him to wear the attire given to TVP front counter employees. The volunteer knew of his 'importance' to the station, refusing all overtures to wear merely an identification badge. The inspector, needing to keep the station open, decided not to rock the boat. Eventually, after receiving a letter from the chief superintendent in charge of local policing the volunteer reluctantly agreed to stop wearing the apparel. This did not solve the problem. He took the garments to his residence after refusing to hand them back. Confrontationally he then purchased a blue shirt, blue tie and dark trousers, in effect replacing the withdrawn attire with his own 'look alike' clothes. Stress levels were high as you can imagine. He was taking on the organisation in a caviller fashion. This over confidence eventually backfired, when his abusive attitude to the local female supervisor, led to potential charges of discrimination. Rather than face such ignominy he resigned and convinced the local papers to print his side of the story. The police did not respond. The unsavoury episode terminated after an officer visited him to recover the bib and tucker. What a mess. Why had it happened? Well, people who proffer their services still need managing and given too much latitude, some will build into their assigned task. He certainly did this.

Officers working on information received, raided a cottage and discovered cannabis plants in the bedroom of a young man whose mother happened to be a volunteer at the same station as the constables involved. Given the tricky situation, she received instructions to stay away, until resolution of the case. She wrote to the chief constable to explain that her parrot, in flight, had dropped cannabis containing bird food in the living quarters causing the plants to grow. Not surprisingly, this extraordinary explanation failed to change opinions. In the end, the son pleaded guilty, prompting his parent to resign.

Eighty-five-years young, an ex RAF pilot, was reported by a serving policewoman for sexual harassment, his touchy feely approach causing offence. He fainted upon hearing the accusation surprised his 'friendliness' had been misconstrued. He subsequently apologised for his unconscious action and the complaint withdrawn.

In 2012, Dorney Reach hosted the Olympic rowing event. A number of volunteers agreed to chauffeur competitors from their hotel to the course. What they did not know is that they would have to pass a very elementary test to confirm competency, even though they held a full licence. One dropped out immediately, another failed an eyesight test but the final embarrassment fell to an elderly volunteer who in manoeuvring the vehicle toward the car park exit, demonstrated such poor ability that he was asked to stop driving before even making the road!

PSVs will do the strangest of things. Many commit to a regular pattern of hours, whilst others provide a helping hand on a when needed basis. This was the case in an exercise drill where, following an imagined nuclear bomb, they were required to feign death at a local train station. Fifty prone volunteers lay along the platform, emergency personnel in attendance, as the train stopped. The majority of unsuspecting alighting commuters, tired after a day's work, did not even break step, stepping over the bodies then walking off as if nothing had happened.

Six PSVs turned up to a Home Office exercise, to act as survivors of a nuclear holocaust. As instructed, they changed into swimming costumes in anticipation of a soaking. Although the seventh person forgot her kit, she merely stripped off to her bra and panties. As the volunteers emerged from a sequence of warm power showers, firefighters wearing head to toe protective gear sprayed them with foam to simulate the cleansing process. All the 'victims' enjoyed the strange experience, none more so than the woman participating in her underwear. She admitted having a thing for firefighters, delighted to report that when out of their safety clothing, they were even better looking than she had imagined. A volunteer dating agency potential maybe?

A young man confessed to his father that he had tragically killed a woman, involved in law enforcement, on a first night date. They went to the local station where the son admitted to killing an off duty policewoman. It turned out the slain person was a PSV, not an officer.

There is no PSV upper age limit. Recently three ninety-year-olds volunteers received long service awards from TVP. Remarkable.

## Steve Moves to Hastings

As soon as Steve was able, he read comics cover to cover that encouraged him to use his fantastic ability to draw cartoons and create his own story lines. He loved Star Trek and particularly Doctor Who, his passion for the Time Lord continuing even today. Whilst at school he appeared in many plays, notably Friar in Romeo and Juliet and Mole in Toad of Toad Hall. He had little interest in playing competitive sport but enjoyed watching it on TV with his brothers. Very talented at writing and playing music he spent hours developing this skill. Recently two of his compositions have featured in audio products by third parties. To earn extra pocket money, he worked in a local greengrocers shop, remaining in the retail trade all his working life.

After graduating from Exeter University, he stayed in Devon for two years before moving back to Reading. He married Andrea and lived in Tilehurst until their divorce. Beth, his lovely daughter, born in Royal Berks hospital on 19 May 1997, now lives in Sheffield.

In 2005, he moved from Reading to Hastings, to live with his partner Helene and her daughter Alice. On 28 July 2010, the birth of their delightful son Jack made the family complete.

In a claim to fame dinner question, Steve would probably choose from the following.

He is the moderator of the 'Sacrifice' Gary Numan web site.

His replica painting of Mondrian's 'composition with red, blue and yellow' still adorns his old bedroom wall; thirty years after its composition...it is that good.

## Mom's Last Resting Place

Toward the end of her life, Mom's mind remained as sharp as a tack, despite blindness in one eye and deteriorating sight in the other. Troubled by blepharitis, she walked with a stick but friends at 'The Chestnuts' looked out for her, running errands, making sure she knew of any evening entertainment, particularly when Betty, the person on the stairs during her initial visit, played the organ. Her neighbour Margaret called in each evening at nine, to share a bedtime drink with her friend. They were a wonderful kind crowd and it was reassuring to know that Mom's last resting place would be with such engaging personalities, in a place so well run by James Butchers and Christine.

> *I never cease to wonder at the kindness of my Chestnut friends,*
> *The little things they do for me go on and it never ends.*
> *But of course it is not only for me, we do it for one another,*
> *Just like a sister or a brother.*
> *We are just like a family and we are all in the same boat,*
> *We stick together in order to keep afloat.*

*If we get into stormy waters, an S.O.S. is passed around,*
*And if it can be done, a life belt arrives to get us on safe ground.*
*When everyone is so kind to me, why do I get all choky,*
*And why does my voice go all croaky?*
*Writing it down has helped, now my heart can sing,*
*Oh! I am just a soft old thing.*

Every Sunday, Mom would join Mary and me to enjoy a traditional roast at Perth Close. February 1, 2009, was no different. Her normal happy self, we had no inclination it would be the last occasion we would see her alive. In hindsight, several odd things happened in the day, which could lead to the conclusion she had an epiphany. After lunch, she removed her hearing aid and lay down on the couch. Normally she would catnap sitting in a chair. This time, after sleeping for two hours she immediately chastised me for playing down achievements. She had never said this as strongly before. Always, when dropping her back at she would leave me by saying.

"Thank you for a lovely day."

On this day she started.

"Thank you for..."

Then after a short hesitation, instead of finishing with her normal words, went on to say.

"...all the things you constantly do for me."

When she went to bed, she said to her friend Margaret.

"My chest is tight. Do not be surprised if I press the button tonight."

When she left Perth Close, her breathing was normal.

At about 7am on the morning after (Monday 2 February) as predicted, she pulled the emergency chord in her room. The call centre in Guildford rang to report they had lost contact with her half way through the conversation. They indicated it might be grave. Regrettably, six inches of snow had fallen during the night, making the journey to her apartment five minutes longer than normal. The ambulance had already arrived. Two paramedics standing inside the hall looked sullen as they conveyed the news I feared...Mom had died. Even though her great age made her vulnerable, it still came as a massive shock. She had been a rock, a stalwart, an inspiration. I felt numb. Thirty minutes later, finally composed, I went into the bedroom to find my beautiful courageous mother at peace. I kissed her gently on the cheek, saying the last goodbyes. I did not linger, emotions high, tears flowing. It appears that Mom, suffering from shortage of breath pulled the emergency cord. She stopped mid-sentence shortly after starting to relate her problem. The telephonist then heard a thud. The medical team arrived at 7.06am to find her on the floor, the receiver trailing. It is reasonable to assume she died the instant she stopped talking and fell.

Mary battled her way through the snow, providing much needed solace. I thought I had prepared for this day, but the devastating impact drained every bit of energy. I kept thinking, my mother, so brave, so loving, was no longer. By luck,

Christine the manager provided the name of a most marvellous funeral director, Richard Lloyd. He arrived at 10am, calm, caring, sympathetic. He quietly removed the body and in a wonderfully soft comforting voice confirmed, he would take good care of her. In the bedroom, we found a red rose on the pillow where Mom had been lying. This type of charming touch continued throughout the whole funeral process.

The flat now so empty had an eerie feeling. Tidy, clean as ever, everything in its proper place but so silent. On the table by the window, a box where Mom often kept her musings lay open. Sitting on top, a verse hand written, finished not polished.

*All mothers are proud of their boys,*
*Achievements when small were rewarded with sweets or toys.*
*One day when Terry was a little boy he gave me quite a start,*
*When he told me his ambition was to drive a dust cart.*
*Carrying a bin on each shoulder was his aim,*
*Oh, yes he thought it would be a great game.*
*But as the years went by, he changed his mind,*
*And chose work of a different kind.*
*And it is something I will never forget,*
*The day he became a Police Cadet.*
*He once came home with blisters on his backside,*
*After his very first police horse ride.*
*But then, after all is said and done,*
*A policeman's lot is not a happy one.*
*For his volunteering he has picked up awards and I am so proud,*
*And I feel like shouting it out loud.*
*But of course, that can't be done,*
*For every mother is proud of her son.*
*So instead of shouting it out loud,*
*He will read this and know that I am proud.*

How poignant, how kind. It had a calming effect to know she had been actively pursuing her vocation right up until the end.

The following day on the way to Asda, an ambulance blue lights flashing, passed our car on the opposite side of the road. I noticed the driver as one of the team who attended to Mom the day before. Fifteen minutes later in the supermarket, I turned to see in civilian clothes, the other paramedic. We instantly embraced as she gently offered her condolences again. What are the odds of seeing not one but both, within 24 hours of such a sad occasion? A message? I do not know, but it provided amazing reassurance.

Four weeks later, Richard the funeral director, walked slowly in front of the hearse as it left Perth Close and later as it passed 'The Chestnuts.' Those residents not attending the funeral were outside the building paying their last respects. In absolute despair, I could not look.

A vicar recommended by Richard conducted the service at Easthamstead Cemetery, Wokingham. Chris, Simon (who had travelled from the Antipodes) Stephen and Duncan (her grandson from Keith's side) stood in front of the congregation bravely eulogising about their grandmother. Unable to control emotions as they said their fond farewells, I bowed my head weeping and remained in this state until the vicar started to talk about life, the hereafter. At last, I felt able to stand up straight, look ahead, join in the hymns. Chas and Dave singing 'Mustn't Grumble' heralded the end of the service. As we left, every close family member gently placed a red rose (and a pink rose for each great-grandchild) on top of the coffin, the final farewell to a much-loved person.

NOTE: Mustn't Grumble, chosen by Steve, could not have been more appropriate. As well as a phrase often used, she sang along to the Chas and Dave album on that last Sunday afternoon.

We celebrated mother's life appropriately at 'The Chestnuts,' among all the friends she had made in the last years of her life. Shortly after arriving, composure regained, I recited my tribute.

> *To Mom,*
> *People will always remember you with a smile,*
> *You always seemed to make everything appear worthwhile,*
> *That's because you cared so much,*
> *You had such a tender touch.*
> *I never thought of you as blind,*
> *Because you were so perceptive and kind.*
> *I never thought of you as hard of hearing*
> *Because you had such instinct, such feeling.*
> *And being an angel you are now at rest in heaven I know,*
> *And if I look to the sky I am sure I will see a warm glow.*
> *You will be sorely missed, you were a treasure,*
> *Your humour, optimism and verses gave so much pleasure.*
> *You were a beautiful person who loved laughter and fun.*
> *I am so proud to have been your son.*

A few weeks later, mother's four great grandchildren released balloons in her memory. We had all now said our last adieu to a special person. She had endured the war, the separation from my father, isolation, Jack's Alzheimer's, her disabilities and in spite of this, her enthusiasm for life remained throughout. Forever able to put an optimistic spin on everything her gentle nature could turn tough when necessary. She ran away from nothing, loved her family and friends passionately. She made an

impact...a mentor... a listener...able to combine humility with the ability to see good in everyone.

A little flowerbed in the garden is the small but constant tribute to my lovely mother.

The wonderful messages of sympathy received from far and near helped overcome the pain. I gathered all of her 'new' work to discover she had indeed written over a hundred poems since the original publication. Consequently, in celebration of her life I decided to publish another volume. At one hundred and twenty nine pages long, dedicated to her memory, 'Verses to Remember Me By,' has the most wonderful cover designed by Melina. Fittingly, the handwritten poem found in Mom's flat after she died is on the final page. All the family have copies; local friends were happy to purchase at cost price and it is available at local libraries and on Amazon.

Two years after her death, I unexpectedly received the most wonderful E-mail from a person I do not know, proving mother's legacy will live forever.

*'Dear Mr. Wilkins, I thought you would like to know I visit a lady who has had a stroke which has affected the vocal chords and as we cannot chat much I read her poems and having practically exhausted all the books of poems in the library, by chance, I picked up Eileen Ridgers 'Verses to remember me by'. She has enjoyed them so much and so have I reading them. To bring a*

*smile to her face is reward enough. Thank you for collating and publishing.'*

## Top Brass

In May 2010, at Windsor Castle, Deputy Chief Constable Chris Lee received the Queens Police Medal. The day before, he and his wife Jo, were kind enough to invite Mary and me to Cliveden for afternoon tea. Of course, I tried to make capital by telling him, the accolade was associated with his involvement in the PSV programme. I mean thirty-five years' service, chairing an anti-terrorist committee, having two bravery citations is not enough for such recognition is it? You need involvement in volunteering, to clinch the deal!

He retired to the New Forest in 2011. An astute leader, he had the foresight to pick a workhorse and enough confidence to let me drive the programme with minimum interference. It seemed an appropriate time to stand down, but after meeting his successor, Deputy Chief Constable Rob Beckley, from Avon and Somerset, I changed my mind. His new 'Citizens in Policing' portfolio included both PSV and Neighbourhood Watch, enabling a more holistic view of the collective potential offered by volunteers. Rob's vision in addition to his creative thinking was irresistible. He assigned one of his staff officers, Mark a sergeant, to the portfolio, in support of my new role, Citizens in Policing Programme Manager.

In 2012, I accepted an invitation from Mark to accompany him and his family to Silverstone to watch the Formula 1 Grand Prix over a three-day period without knowing the arrangements. With five days to go, Mark rang. I thought that at first he was having a laugh when he said I needed to bring a tent. I had assumed we would be staying in a hotel. On the Friday opening day of the scheduled three, with a tent stowed in the boot of the car, I did not even make it. Torrential rain made driving problematical so I turned back on advice from Mark who arrived in Silverstone after an eight-hour journey from Bristol! On the Saturday qualifying day, I arrived at the waterlogged quagmire of a campsite at 7am. Mark complained he had endured a dreadful night, his unkempt appearance tending to confirm this actuality, whilst his wife Jo on the other hand looked cool, calm and collected. We all trudged up a flooded rural road seduced by the roar of the racing cars in practice. In a grandstand, we huddled together in swirling winds, the rain ceaseless. As they fought for grid position, the drivers exhibited amazing skill. The screaming, screeching rockets with a passing noise per car of one hundred and forty seven decibels demanded attention. They could have been robots though. I did not see anyone get into the car and the static figure in the cockpit barely moved.

"How do I know it is really Lewis Hamilton in the McLaren car?"

"By his yellow helmet!"

After the end of the qualification session, freezing cold, soaking wet, we made our way slowly back. I looked around the bedraggled campsite, at the excuse of a toilet, deciding there and then not to pitch my tent in the quagmire. Mark and his family understood, obviously not wanting to see a grown man cry. I did not return on Sunday either. In the end, I watched the race, amazingly run in full sunshine, from the comfort of the living room. Whilst an interesting experience and a delight to meet Mark's family, I will in future, leave television to prove it is indeed Hamilton in the yellow helmet propelling his monster round the track.

This was not the first time accommodation had proved demanding when travelling with Mark. The Home Office allowance of £100 for an overnight stay in London ensured few people took advantage of this generosity! The last hotel frequented left much to be desired. A tiny (could not swing a cat around in it) room, linked directly to a ranch type door, overlooked a main road and adjoined a lift. Continual road noise and people returning to their rooms guaranteed lack of sleep, the poor T.V. reception offering no respite. Continental breakfast in the basement, offered the massive choice of orange juice, cornflakes, slice of cheese, hard-boiled eggs, bread and marmalade. Accessed via the lift outside my room, this dingy room decorated with circles of brown gloss paint, could have been a replica of the Maze prisoner excesses. Mark, responsible for booking this accommodation deserved the considerable stick from yours truly. Conceivably, snoozing in a tent on wet ground at Silverstone would have been preferable to this experience in London.

After a year, Mark obtained a well-earned promotion to inspector. Lee a bright, hardworking talented constable took his place. In November 2012, Police and Crime Commissioners (PCCs) replaced police authorities. Elected by the community, PCCs control the purse strings, holding the chief constable to account. They are likely to embrace volunteering as a method of improving links with the community, providing extra capacity. The concerning question is whether attempts will be made to politicise the police. John Prescott put himself forward as a PCC candidate so you can see why I am concerned.

Most of the police service organisations now accept PSV's as a valuable added value resource and I am proud to have contributed. Mary thought I devoted too much time to the position and she had a point. What started small grew to a level where significant time was required to fulfil the function but I found it difficult to compromise. My philosophy has always been 'if you intend to do something, do it well'. During the process of developing the national approach, I received fantastic encouragement and endorsement from employee practitioners doubling as PSV regional representatives. Like most these days, they did not really have any spare capacity, yet they were able to find a little extra when requested. Recently, I have been fortunate to secure the voluntary services of Bob Johnson, a friend and retired 3M colleague. If he so desires, Bob can continue to assist the national portfolio, long after I have left. For sure, he is a great addition to the team.

*'The Prime Minister has asked me to inform you, <u>in strict confidence</u>, that having accepted the advice of the Head of the Civil Service and the Main Honours Committee, he proposes to submit your name to the Queen. He is recommending that Her Majesty may be graciously pleased to approve that you be appointed an Officer of the Order of the British Empire in the 2012 Birthday Honours List'.*

The words in a letter from the Cabinet Office did not register at first. After the third reading, it finally dawned on me what it meant. Celebrities often receive such a title but a man born in Hay Mills? Proud and humbled my heart beat excitedly as I hugged Mary.

At Buckingham Palace on 9 November 2012, the Queen gently pinned the OBE medal to my morning suit, in recognition of my

services to the police. With Mary, Steve, Simon and Chris watching it made the event even more special. A once in a lifetime experience, taking everything in was impossible. The surroundings, ambiance, paintings, formality, building; the whole thing. I had tried to appear cool but this was impossible. Others, clearly felt the same way. As we waited in line to be presented, I turned to a woman recipient behind me.

"Not long now. I feel very nervous."

"So do I" she retorted.

"I feel better to know I am not the only one."

"Yes, except I do not know why I'm apprehensive because I work for the Queen. I am one of her three secretaries. I talk to her all the time."

"It must be the occasion."

"I have helped with these ceremonies before. Never did I dream the Queen would give me a title."

The words expressed by the Queen's secretary illustrate perfectly the sense of occasion.

Steve's Facebook blog superbly captured the whole experience.

*"The last few days all felt slightly surreal.*
*Staying at one of the oldest hotels in London, in five star luxury and then being whisked to Buckingham Palace to see my Dad get his O.B.E from Her Majesty the Queen.*
*Actually walking through the gates of the Palace, I felt like a celebrity. The fences surrounding the building are always lined with tourists and, because we were all dressed up to the nines and were actually inside the Palace courtyard, people were taking our photos! Very bizarre. And it felt really odd to look back and see them all peering through the railings at you.*
*And then to go through the entrance of the building, into an inner courtyard, that I had seen on TV at William and Kate's wedding, was incredible. We then entered the Palace itself and were greeted with incredibly ornate architecture and guards in their gleaming Horse Guard's*

uniforms. There were several at the entrances to each of the regal staircases, some in gold armour and some in silver. It was spine tingling. Unfortunately, we were made to give in all of our cameras and mobile phones as there were strict rules of no photography within the Palace itself.

Before being ushered through a long hallway to the Ballroom, I decided to use one of the toilets, just to say that I had done it! The facilities were posh, but nothing too grand, but then I guess we were using the plebs toilets.

Once in the Ballroom, we were seated by the ushers, resplendent in their

uniforms. By this time, Dad was waiting with the other recipients in another room.

The Ballroom, we were told, is used for numerous state functions and was ornate in gold and marble, with columns and buttresses, huge paintings and a spotless red carpet. And, at the back of a raised dais at the

far end, were two thrones, both decked in gold. They were flanked on each side by Yeoman of the Guard, looking amazing in their red beefeater uniforms. And these were not young men and they stood, with heavy staffs, at least 10 feet high, for over two hours, never flinching. Incredible! We were given a brief overview of the history of the ceremony and the *room itself and then, at 11.00 am sharp, the Queen arrived from the right of the room. We all stood and the National Anthem was played by a string quartet. She then told us we could sit. We were about 30 feet from her and she is really tiny!*

*The various people receiving gongs, arrived one by one, announced each time, by award, name and the reason for the recognition. We saw Kenneth Branagh receive his Knighthood, kneeling before the Queen as she used an ancient sword, used since the 1400's, on each shoulder. Other recipients received gallantry medals, Victoria's Crosses, MBE's CBE, etcetera. etcetera.*

*And, of course, there was the moment when my father walked in, stood before Her Majesty and she pinned his OBE to his chest. Never have I felt prouder of anything in my life. Myself, my two bothers and my Mum were literally bursting with pride.*

*The Queen spoke to every recipient and Dad said that she asked about his work with the Police, for which he was receiving the award, how it was going and how many volunteers he had. After their brief chat, my father said that she gently took his hand again and very subtly pushed him away, her way of saying that he needed to move back to make way for the next person.*

*What a moment. One that we will never forget and certainly, for my father, will always be one of the highlights of his life.*

*After the ceremony was complete, we went back out in the inner courtyard and had some professional photographs taken and took some ourselves, many of which I have posted on Facebook, which I know some of you have already seen.*

*A quite incredible couple of days and, like I said, it all seems a bit surreal, once you get back to the humdrum of real life.*

*And here I am now, typing this back in my little house in Hastings. The proudest son on the planet (apart from the other two proudest sons of course!)*

On leaving the Palace in full morning suit, tourists milled

around curious to find out the occasion. A Japanese couple wanted a joint photo. An American wanted to know in which conflict I had fought. I missed a trick; I should have said the First World War!

After the most marvellous, never to be forgotten occasion, we travelled to Hastings. At Steve and Helene's abode, over a drink we talked about the day, before retiring, the boys kipping in sleeping bags on the couch. Back to the real world.

Late in 2012, the newly established College of Policing, replaced NPIA. Bob Johnson and I became their first volunteers two years later but our responsibilities remained the same. Time will tell if more will follow.

In the next twenty years, the nature of policing in the UK will change. Austerity will demand new approaches to deliver services. Volunteers will play an increasing part whether directly managed or self-motivated. PSVs will be an integral part of a 'Citizen in Policing' approach that, under guidance from the authorities, will look at holistic ways that social action, can help make communities safer.

At the end of March 2015, recognising the need to reduce my hours, I moved out of mainstream national day-to-day coordination of the programme, but remained a board member of the Citizens in Policing Community of Practice (CiPCoP). This facilitated, in June 2016, my appointment as the first Citizens in Police Ambassador for Thames Valley Police. It is my intention to stay involved nationally and locally until I lose enthusiasm or my ability to add value. When this happens, I hope police colleagues will think of me as a person who made a lasting contribution to policing and the community.

## Holidays

Retirement has been good. Mary is my best friend. We still have good health, are able to enjoy life to the full and enjoy as many sabbaticals as funds will allow.

Incredibly, the Bilbao ferry fiasco did not dampen our sea fearing enthusiasm. We embarked on our maiden cruise to the Fiords of Norway aboard the Saga Rose, a magnificent well-appointed ship. The waiters from the Philippines were superb, food and shore excursions excellent, but not all was perfect. Although we were in our mid-fifties we were amongst the youngest of four hundred passengers. The blurb said the cruise suited the over fifties whilst in reality it catered merely for the over seventies. I marvelled at the way the older generation coped with the vagaries of a ship, but two died during the seven days and had Mary not helped a woman she found suffering from shortness of breath, it could have been three! Entertainment was dull, the bored band repeating their slow playlist each evening doing nothing to attract 'youngsters.' For many, the zimmer-frame waltz became their crowning moment.

Suffering considerable pain from a gum abscess, I reluctantly visited the ship's medical quarters to find a large man in a white coat, standing in the doorway to the surgery.

"Once you cross this threshold," he boomed, "it will cost you thirty-five pounds, so be sure you need to."

He eventually prescribed antibiotics and I naively asked if it would still be okay to have a drink.

"Good God man, of course you can! Everyone imbibes on a ship."

This larger than life man turned out to have been the Chief Medical Officer during the Falklands War, Rick Jolly, the doctor who attended to Simon Weston. His talk in the ballroom proved to be the highlight of the week. His stories were humorous and truly inspirational. He controversially believed in open wound healing and allowing injured soldiers to self-administer morphine from a phial provided by him. After the conflict, he received a most extraordinary double honour. An OBE from the

Queen and the equivalent from the Argentine government for saving the lives of many of their soldiers. A remarkable person,

The breath taking scenery of the Fiords provided a magnificent backdrop, whetting our appetite to undertake such ventures again. We decided in future to travel on ships catering for a variety of ages. Since then, we have voyaged to places as far

afield as St. Petersburg, Egypt, Caribbean and Alaska proving the Bilbao taster trip was not a disaster after all.

Competitively priced cruising is now available to all, making the first night's dining experience interesting. We normally opt to sit on a table of six to eight, happy to mingle. Meeting fellow diners without any knowledge of their background or eminence can create a dynamic atmosphere. We try to keep an open mind though it can be testing.

On an early cruise, an Irish family chatted about everyday things their quiet lullaby voices mesmerising. The husband of the other couple on the table boasted of his exploits in winning the Burma war single-handed, his upper crust condescending accent nauseous. My blood boiled at his dismissive attitude and his outrageous self-aggrandisement. I resorted to the lowest form of wit...sarcasm. Something had to give. The following night the 'plumb in the mouth' couple, gleefully announced they had found a more suitable table by a window with a nice class of people and would not be returning! The neck, the cheek, but if they were happy we were ecstatic. For the remainder of the cruise we enjoyed our dinners with the Irish family. We did not see the war hero couple again. Given the status they crave, we are unlikely to meet them again. I hope they are satisfied with their lot.

On the second night of a more recent cruise, we went to dinner expecting to find six of the original eight passengers at the table. As predicted the military couple, another pair of snobs, failed to return, but unexpectedly, neither did the London bendy bus driver and his partner, an East End cafe owner. The remaining couple from Wales, Renee and Terry, were stoic. We laughingly agreed to join each other at the dinner table every evening to save the embarrassment of two sitting at a table for eight. On the third day, we bumped into the East End couple. Their intense dislike of the military couple and the need to consume more bulk than fine dining could provide had driven them to eat in the self-service restaurant. They joined the table twice more, regaling all with their winning down to earth, cockney humour. What a pity they felt so awkward earlier on. I guess cruising reflects human nature. With up to four thousand living as neighbours, it would be rare for a few not to feel aggravated.

During the period on board, it is easy to make casual acquaintances. Occasionally guests become permanent friends. We met Ray and Ann on a Caribbean trip, joining them on their table at the suggestion of the headwaiter. I am so pleased we did. They are a super, fun loving couple who live in Aberdeen a mere four-hundred miles away! On our second evening together, Ray, a large imposing figure, asked if we would join him at karaoke, not our favourite pastime. We were pleasantly surprised when a gentle melodic voice emanated from such a large man. Sinatra would have been proud. I have little doubt we have made life-long friends, even after an interesting visit to a coffee bar in Stockholm. The camp waiters, the paintings of men copulating should have provided a clue. We finally twigged, after noticing risqué magazines on the floor featuring the male gender. I wonder what impression the waiters formed of a bald headed man, a large Scotsman and two petite women in a cafe for gay people. Telling our story later, other guests expressed amazement at our naïve blindness in failing to notice the rainbow flag outside the establishment. We met Trisha and Keith later. They live in Chard, Somerset. Keith became besotted with Linda Lusardi, travelling on the ship accompanied by her husband, Sam Kane, a headline act. I did not understand the fascination. After all, she did not win the vote as the top page three girl off all time, finishing only third! Keith repeatedly ordered 'two scoops' of ice cream with his dessert, so this became his nickname.

It is possible in a short period to be on nodding or speaking terms with many people. In a small canapés bar, we tried to communicate with a Russian woman. I will call her Leyla. Waving hands, mouthing words did not help. In the end, with translation via a casino employee, we learned she moved in high circles. Her best friend being Putin's maid.

'Soul mates' now, pecks on the cheek were exchanged if we saw each other around the ship. Comfortable in her own skin

Layla would often shake her bits on the dance floor in splendid isolation. She moved well for a heavy person, the rolls of fat swaying gently in unison with her every body movement. To me though it seemed sad. Alone on the ship. Alone on the dance floor. We were now mates so one night on a whim, I decided to join her. I announced my arrival by loud, matador style stamping. Having noticed such a splendid entrance, she moved toward me as I pretended to swish an imaginary cape. She caught on directly - they are bright these Russians. She lowered her head, brushing past my svelte body as I teased the oncoming bull. By now, aware of a 'special event' in their presence, spectators started to shout encouragement. I strutted around, bent right arm in the air, the left behind my arched back, clicking fingers, an invite for the bull to attack again. She obliged and in a quick, rather than passionate swift movement, I pulled her generous body to mine before pushing her away, in an exaggerated masculine manner. Leyla merrily waved goodbye, enjoying the standing ovation. Mary smiled warmly; relieved no doubt, that guests had enjoyed the 'performance.'

Moreover, the story does not end there. The witnesses to the dance spectacle offered sincere greetings as we visited our favourite little bar the following evening. The charming barman produced a greeting card with a photograph of a rather portly woman on the front, remarkably similar to my foreign dance partner. Inside, a message written in Russian. When Leyla arrived, following a hug, I pointed to the words, nodding, in an effort to convey thanks for her kind thoughts in buying me a card. Unexpectedly, she grabbed the card, pulling it to her ample bosom. Slapping a big kiss on my cheek, not merely a peck, she hurried to the exit, clutching 'her' trophy. A surprising symphony of raucous laughter followed when a guest admitted asking the interpreter to write a few appropriate Russian words to thank **me** for the previous evening's entertainment. As the one person able to understand the message, we all wondered why Leyla had been so pleased. The instigator of the plot disappeared to find the author of the words. She returned beaming. 'It said you are a lovely dancer. Be happy.' That explained everything.

A ship is full of great characters. In a lift, a tall greying middle-aged guest, accompanied by a young Taiwanese woman acquiesced as I joined them with a "good morning" and a nod.

"I know what you're thinking," he said. I shrugged my shoulders.

"No, I did not bring her back from the Far East; I met her in a Chinese restaurant in London." He had a cheeky knowing smile on his face.

"She looks after me great but when she invites me upstairs for sex, I tell her I am only able to do one thing at a time!"

What an introduction. He was an ex Scotland Yard detective who battled with the Krays in their heyday. He now owned a company appointed to ensure correct administration of the license agreement between Sky and the premier league. He told many interesting, potentially inflammatory stories. A most entertaining man with a patter to match, I reckon he had his life sorted.

It could be that the saying, once a copper, always a copper is actually true, as I would often meet passengers who had been in the job. Over breakfast, a retired copper from Newcastle once more illustrated the bizarre humour of people within the emergency services. He said a dead body washed up from the Tyne would often be stored in a small police office to await collection. If new wide-eyed recruits were around, directed to the 'morgue' by colleagues, on opening the door they would find the corpse sitting upright on a stored pedal cycle.

## So Much More

Visiting the theatre and watching live performances are a major part of our leisure. We have seen many superstars. Elton John, Bryan Adams, Shania Twain, Rod Stewart, Kenny Rogers, Eagles, Sir Cliff Richard and the Shadows. We have a few artists left on our bucket list. Robbie Williams and Michael Buble' for Mary. I would settle again, for a jaw dropping forty-year-old Tina Turner, arriving on stage in a shimmering silver mini-skirt right up to her armpits. In a trance, I apparently salivated. What a star.

Joining HPB has proved to be a sensible investment. On one occasion, we decided to participate in an HPB watercolour theme week at St. Brides Castle in Pembrokeshire. It turned out to be an interesting, inspirational vacation, which may explain why I chose the experience as a suitable subject for an HPB writing competition. The piece 'Painting by Accident' remarkably gained second place resulting in the presentation of a Mont Blanc pen. I knew the story would be interesting, but never felt confident I had the ability to translate it into the written word. You can make up your own mind if I succeeded.

*"It is difficult to know the logic behind why my wife and I attended a watercolour theme week at St. Brides back in 1999. After all, a man and wife attending a theme week should have similar interests, shouldn't they? Well, yes, but in our case, not true.*

*Whilst Mary, my wife, was skilled at drawing and painting exquisite flowers, my artistic skill level was below a small child. Even a game of Pictionary was challenging. I could not even draw stick men well enough for anyone to guess what I was trying to convey and for some reason, those same stick men always had triangular heads. Why, is something you would have to ask a psychologist.*

*So why did I go? Well I guess it is the married, doing things together,, building brownie points. Importantly, I also had a Master Contingency Plan (MCP)......a set of golf clubs in the boot of the car....with Mary's agreement of course. My expectation was that I would attend initially, apologise and then leave Mary to continue to improve her skills while I enjoyed the hospitality of the local golf courses. Sheer genius, I thought.*

*And my plan nearly worked! On the first day, I sat close to my wife at the back of the room - on the basis I was less likely to be found out - and listened to all the other participants outline their artistic ability. I was amazed at the standard the students were already producing. One person, I swear, was as good as Constable! His clouds were amazing! Another had painted the view from her window...apparently she had dashed it off the night before! I had to be honest and stated my skill level was zero. I mentioned my Pictionary experience. Some people sniggered. Others just sat and looked at me. I felt inadequate.*

*The instructors, Joy and Shirley were not at all fazed by my plight. They quickly confirmed the course was designed to suit all skill levels, even those without any skills at all! I liked them. They were a bit like French and Saunders. Shirley jovial and happy go-lucky whilst Joy was more studious and methodical. They were very sympathetic to my plight. They continually encouraged me to try the things they were suggesting and then told untruths by saying I was making progress. They must have realised my discomfort, as they were even kind enough to laugh at the dreadful humour I was attempting in order to hide my ineptitude. So on the evening of the first day, I was sure six hours of being an artist would be enough to last me a lifetime and that the MCP would come into operation.*

*I am not sure why I decided to expose myself to another eight hours of purgatory, but I did. The weather was good. I could have played golf but decided that quitting (and after paying all that money) would be difficult to rationalise and would give my mates back home a field day when they found out (which they definitely would...need I say more). At least my colleagues now knew I was useless. My efforts to produce anything meaningful continued to be woeful and it was clear I would be the only student without a painting in the exhibition planned for the last day. I remember Joy coming to look at my attempt to draw a sheep and bursting out laughing before instantly apologising to the class saying, "I know tutors should not laugh at students work but just look at this!" I laughed with her, in order to hide my embarrassment at having produced a living animal, which looked like a demented robot. But this episode, in a strange way, actually lightened my stress levels and that of my fellow students. It was now clear when I said I could not draw I was actually telling the truth. I was ready to throw the towel in yet again. But fellow students rallied to my defence, "We'll miss you if you go, you're funny. You make us laugh." This show of emotional blackmail was very touching but I was aware the purists wanted me to do the honourable thing and go and play golf.*

*However, given my newly acquired status as the 'Entertainment Officer' I felt very relieved and surprisingly decided to stay the course. I have always believed that one should be able to laugh at oneself and on this stage, I was able to prove it.*

*Then something happened. It was early on day three. It was not so much a miracle but more an awakening. Wet on Wet arrived. This watercolour process meant I could now produce a picture without really knowing what I was doing! I loved it. I found I was quite capable of wetting the paper with water, adding colour and then watch it being miraculously absorbed and spread according to where it wanted to go not where I tried to put it. Painting by accident! Brilliant! Real artists reading this will understandably now be agitated, for I know I have trivialised, simplified and ridiculed an accepted watercolour process. I can only apologise and ask them to understand even if Wet on Wet is far more sophisticated than I have explained, it made me, for the first time, want to pick up a paint brush. No mean task.*

*The last two days thus became more enjoyable and rewarding. I felt reinforced. I stopped messing around and became a model student (well almost!) I started to take an interest in techniques and colour patterns. I still felt useless but at least now I had some enthusiasm. Joy, bless her, on the day before the exhibition held up two of my attempts. She said, "In my left hand is Terry's effort from day one and in my right hand is the Wet on Wet painting he has just produced. This shows remarkable progress. This is going into the exhibition." And it did. Joy told me, whether truthfully or not, that someone wanted to buy my painting. There was, of course, no way my only worthwhile attempt would go anywhere.... except on the wall of my mother's apartment......no, I did not have to pay her. Now when I go on holiday I take my watercolours as well as my golf clubs. I have completed over fifty paintings (one of St.Brides) and some people (other than my mother) like them enough to hang them on their wall. Whilst Wet on Wet inspired me, I am thankfully, now capable of using other techniques as well. I am grateful to the Theme Week, to Joy and Shirley and the other students for putting up with me and of course my lovely wife, Mary, for persuading me to go." P.S. I am still rubbish at Pictionary.*

The St. Brides HPB property is my attempt to show the

splendour of the building. You can see I am only adequate at the art, unlike my brother Keith, who created the wonderful painting of our mother.

We have enjoyed many vacations with Keith and Alma over the years, travelling to South Africa, Australia and the U.S. On early holidays, we would never stay long in one place, driving to different locations in a superior hire vehicle, the highlight a Lincoln 'Town Car.' Eventually, we opted to stay at a

base for a week or so, before moving on. We were in Vail, Colorado, to celebrate Keith's birthday on July 4 and witnessed the uninhibited exuberance of the Americans to demonstrate pride in their country. The waving of the Stars and Stripes flag, the whooping as the parades passed, the marching bands and an early evening open-air concert by the Boston Philharmonic Orchestra, created a wonderful atmosphere. Returning to our superb log cabin, we sat outside in the Jacuzzi, drinking champagne. A magical day.

While still in the wonderful State of Colorado, we decided to go horse riding at a local dude ranch. It was a brave decision...Mary had never sat astride a donkey let alone a horse; Keith and Alma's experience was limited to a couple of short rides in Palm Springs; My hour-long jaunt on a police horse had left extensive posterior blister damage. On arrival, the owner dressed in full cowboy monty, outlined the morning plan...a two-hour ride through natural countryside. We all needed help to mount the steeds, especially Mary who, assisted by a push, catapulted into the saddle. We set off in a line of five, the cowboy at the front. He explained the horses would follow the leader so we should sit back, enjoy. We gently rode through trees, open scrubland, stopping now and again so the rancher could relate stories about the area. All went well until resting stags jumped up, skittishly running off. The horses freaked a little, Mary hanging on impressively as her mare made as if to rear. After an hour, my derrière started to ache badly, relief impossible, a stiff upper lip the only option. If we stopped, Mary would turn around grimacing. She wanted out. On the other hand, Alma appeared at ease with the whole thing, in spite of following a smelly flatulent horse, whilst Keith in jeans, hat and boots was living the role. Arriving back at base, it did not take a rocket scientist to deduce we were all suffering to varying degrees. Mary remained in the saddle her discomfort obvious. She fell into the arms of the older cowboy as he carefully helped her to the ground. With aching wobbly legs everyone gave their verdict. Alma and Keith said they enjoyed the experience. Mary, not surprisingly, said she would definitely decline another opportunity. I confirmed the end of my riding career. They are the most wonderful animals, so much power, so eager, but perhaps given my experience with 246 Sultan, the saying 'once bitten twice shy' is appropriate.

More typically, Keith and I would play golf on a local course and occasionally at a top venue. In cold biting rain, Pebble Beach, California, ranked the best in America and seventh in the world presented the major challenge. Keith played close to his handicap whilst I found the course and appalling conditions difficult, resulting in a collapse of significant proportions after the tenth hole. Such a fantastic 'big dent in the bank balance' experience, like all great vacations, will stay in the memory forever.

We rack up plenty of miles visiting family down under. Personally, I would be happy to have an injection as I board the plane, put in a tube and sleep until an hour out from the Antipodes. Alas, this is not possible so the next best thing is to make the journey as pain free as possible. While funds allow, we have decided to travel premium economy with no stopovers, best to get it over with all at once. We can then relax and spend quality time with the family. We thoroughly enjoy our visits to the Antipodes but I am constantly anxious I could encounter snakes (in Australia). They scare me and I have been close. Mel's brothers killed a deadly brown snake on the patio of her parents' home in the Blue Mountains, whilst Mary and I remained blissfully unaware of the drama. With Keith and Alma in our hire car, we came across a snake in the middle of the road. It looked dead. Keith very brave, suggested I get out of the car to have a gander. You can imagine my reaction. On the other hand, Mary hates spiders and there are plenty in Australia. On entering our Mosman apartment, she suddenly stopped, pointing at the wall five yards ahead on our right, screaming a little as she did so. A little extreme perhaps, but spread stock-still, an enormous brown spider (leg span at least eight inches) dominated the room with a relaxed spooky intimidating stillness. The size did not concern me but I worried that it could be poisonous. Mary broke the silence.

"I cannot come into the room, until that thing is removed."

Without a solution, I rang Mel (Simon's now ex) trying and I am sure failing to appear unflustered. Calmly she asked.

"Has it got any hairs on its body?"

Did she really think I would know the answer? I moved cautiously toward to the spider, able to see hair on its brown bulbous form.

"It's good news" enthused Mel.

"It is probably a Huntsman. They are big, hairy, not poisonous so relatively harmless, although they do bite."

Far from reassured, the possibly still remained we could be frightened or bitten to death. The spider, obviously sporting for a fight did not move.

"What would you do now Mel?"

"I would zap it with a shoe."

Just another day at the office for my daughter in law, with little recognition of the stress evident in our room.

"OK thanks I'll try."

"Be careful. They have eight eyes and can jump two yards or so."

Black shoe in hand, I slowly crawled toward the spider. When near enough, with pounding heart, I aimed a blow surely accurate enough to end the monster's life. In an instant, the spider leapt forward about five feet, coming to rest on the rear of a television speaker. Mary yelled. Startled, I froze. What now?

"I cannot go to bed until the thing has been killed."

"Thanks. How do you propose I do that? I cannot zap it now, as I might break the speaker and if I miss, it will jump again."

Out of ideas, silence descended. The spider remained in full view, unfazed. Suddenly, Mary took a few steps back, disappeared, returning with a can of hair spray.

"Try this" she said full of optimism...unusual for my wife.

A sarcastic reply nearly spilled out, until on instant reflection, it seemed it could be the solution given the spider did indeed have hair! It did not move, as the spray hit it full blast. Slowly the monster shrivelled into a small ball, no longer a menace. I felt a pang of guilt to witness the destruction of such magnificence but completed the job, squashing it into oblivion with a tissue. I strutted around, anticipating some plaudits. Mary, having none of it, still had survival on her mind.

"Let's hope there are no more lurking around."

The morning after, Mel enquired if all went well. I related the story, trying not to embellish the size of the monster or its enormous leap. She listened politely, not at all impressed by my heroics.

'Well you'll now know what to do next time, won't you?"

## Health Management

Of course, the back will never be perfect. I try to avoid twisting and pulling though it is not easy to think about the 'rules' when instinct dictates otherwise.

The great thing about good friends is they care. Vic knew I had been in trouble for two weeks, lying on a board most of the time. With a wooden chair secured immediately behind the driver's cabin, he and Ian arrived determined to ensure I enjoy the customary Sunday, Lands' End lunchtime pint. They coaxed me from the living room into the vehicle. Vic stood by my side to make sure the chair did not move, whilst Ian drove to the pub. Although edgy, I marvelled at the ingenuity of friends. On arrival, a bit like a Rajah, they carried me on the chair, into the bar, much to the surprise of customers who did not know the history. They repeated the process on the return journey, the anxiety reduced. Alcohol has that effect!

Whilst, recovering from the second back operation, stiff, unable to bend and only raising from the prone position to go to the toilet, Vic visited. He wanted to gate crash the wedding reception of a couple from the Land's End, then read a poem. He asked, not for the first time, if I would accompany him to act as his Dutch courage. Four days later, I struggled into his car. The plan was simple. He would arrive dressed as a sweep and I would follow in cow gown, to clear up the soot he had dropped on the floor. Riveting stuff. The video shows Vic prancing around in front of the married couple whilst a gloomy, very rigid individual, broom in hand, tries to look 'cool' hanging around doing nothing in particular. The event over, I returned to the board, relieved to have survived, pleased with my small part in a special wedding gift.

Whilst I try to 'manage' the spinal issues, when in an intense spasm I have no choice but to start the repair process again. After a short boat trip, I spent an hour lying on an outdoor table in order to make it possible to walk again. In the HQ of Thames Valley Police, medics assisted the wounded soldier before Julie kindly drove me home, following a dictate from an inspector. On a recent plane journey back from Australia, in agony, I rejected the offer of morphine.

Dorothy, a very experienced physiotherapist, now retired, knew exactly what to do if I was in trouble with her magic firm hands. I have arrived in the midst of a spasm and been able to walk away following treatment. For fifteen years, on a prevention basis about four times per year, Dorothy performed her miracles and kept me relatively mobile.

It seems most people have had vertebral problems to some degree. If involved in a conversation with someone who does not know my history, I often say in an earnest tone.

"I have had two discs taken out of my back. I was six foot six tall once. Now I am only six foot."

I love watching the reaction as they compute whether it could be possible, then their relief as I break into a smile and tell them it is not true.

Lately, I have also experienced problems with neck and shoulders. On the recommendation of mate Bob, I decided to visit 'Back in Line' a practice in Henley, experts in treating injuries to rugby players. He raved about the place and on arrival, I understood why. Attractive women specialists were everywhere – it must be in the job description. Suzy, a charming friendly sports massage technician. Amy a registered chiropractor, also a Great Britain equestrian international, adept in treating children and horses. Vivienne the founder who studied advanced acupuncture in China. Recently, after watching the Virgin advert, featuring beautiful air hostesses in red uniforms strutting their stuff through an airport, I could not help thinking that if chiropractors needed similar publicity, they would surely choose this practice. Apparently, there are a couple of men around, but I have not really noticed them!

At the beginning of 2015, I joined the local Virgin Active gym. Addressing the symptom has been a reasonable strategy in maintaining mobility, but in recent years, the need for treatment had become more frequent, so I decided to adopt a different approach. I now visit the Virgin Active in Wokingham two/three times a week and utilise the expertise of personal trainer Rob, who has an intimate understanding of the issues having undergone back surgery himself. I trust his judgement when he moves me from one exercise to another. So far, so good. Early days but all indicators are very positive. My back is stronger, I am fitter and after sixty minutes of activity...treadmill, floor exercises and weights. I enjoy the pleasure of coffee and putting the world to rights with Trevor and Brenda.

## Sport and Games

Whether watching or playing, I have consistently derived great pleasure from the competitive nature of sport

Taking part rather than winning at any cost has always been my key motivation...play competitively, treat defeat and success with grace. I have been fortunate with bat and ball in hand, to possess enough dexterity not to look a fool, average at most though distinguished at none.

Since retiring, golf has been my main sporting activity. I disagree with Mark Twain when he said it was a good walk spoiled because he surely failed to recognise it is a supreme test of technique and a catalyst for building friendships. I never played at 3M HOGS (Head Office Golfing Society) whilst working, but since retirement have fully participated, enabling me to keep in contact with likeminded colleagues, Vyv, Sid and Trevor. Captaining the society one year, I was able to witness the awesome secretarial capabilities of Keith Perkins, master of planning and negotiation. Being a member of Sonning, enabled me to play constantly with low handicap players of my age,

Richard, Bill, Jim, Ken and of course Keith, which undoubtedly improved my game. As they say 'old golfers never die, they just lose their balls.' I now play less than once per week, so a current handicap of thirteen is likely to increase rapidly, unless a miracle happens or I wake up with an entirely new swing. This is unlikely, given that during a lesson many years ago, the professional said he could do nothing to improve my game!

Of course linked to playing sport is the excitement of watching. Television is fine but nothing beats a live event. I have been fortunate to see many...five nation's rugby match at Cardiff Arms Park...cricket at the Oval, Lords and Edgbaston...a Ryder Cup practice day at Celtic Manor. In the States, basketball, American football, baseball and in Australia, the Ashes and rules football. Remaining on the bucket list are Wimbledon, ice hockey, cycling, athletics and then that is it.

## Life Together

My lovely wife is a natural homebuilder as well as a fantastic mother. Well-organised, she habitually seems able to create down time even in the most hectic of circumstances. Division of labour occurred naturally, Mary happy to look after domestic chores whilst I concentrated on building a career. We saved, remaining debt free - with the exception of the mortgage.

I would like to think we have been good parents...setting the right example, supportive and providing sufficient freedom to allow development. We tried to keep disagreements to ourselves, but occasionally failed miserably. Watching television with the boys when of school age created a dilemma for me, if the actors used strong language. This came to a head as we watched Beverley Hills Cop. After about thirty minutes, uneasy at the level and content of swearing I switched off the box, much to the annoyance of the family.

"We hear it all the time in the playground Dad."

A miserable few hours followed. The day after, they watched the film with Mary while I was at work, graphically illustrating the futility of my narrow mind.

Watching football on TV often stimulated debate...a referee's decision, the best team, the most valuable player. I would occasionally make frivolous funny (to me at least) comments about a player's ability based on his place of birth. I should have noticed the boys rarely smiled, as during one session they turned off the TV.

"We think your comments are inherently racist. We do not like it," said Steve, the spokesperson.

I had failed to recognise my offensiveness, yet when pointed out, it was easy to see why the boys were upset.

Mary and I work in partnership. When wallpapering for instance, we will work as a team, loosely analogous to a surgeon performing an operation surrounded by a team of helpers. Instead of a scalpel, scissors would instantly be in my hand when requested or more than likely in a convenient spot, Mary anticipating the need. This has occasionally resulted in personal sacrifice. Decorating the stairs, Mary stood holding a trough full of water and a roll of water activated adhesive paper destined to embellish the longest point of the stair well. Perched high on a ladder I pulled the paper upward toward me, and in so doing, dragged the wet adhesive directly over Mary's face causing her to lose her balance. The liquid in the trough raced free, tipping over the sides, soaking her clothes. From my lofty position, it looked hilarious so I did not restrain laughter. Fortunately, Mary also saw the humorous side.

Throughout our marriage, we have tackled head on any major issues, always with the intention we would solve the problem. Mary has coped with my complexities and quirkiness with remarkable fortitude, flexibility and understanding. I love my wife dearly and I know the feeling is mutual. I could not have wished for a more beautiful, loving soul mate. During our golden wedding anniversary year, we celebrated by flying Simon, Chris and their families to England so that with Steve and his menage we could all be together again. It could not have been a happier time. Our sons, their wives, partners and nine lovely grandchildren.

## Letters Patent

It arrived in a brilliant red box emblazoned with the Queen's Crest. My own coat of arms granted under crown authority by letters patent, designed and painted by master craftsmen on vellum parchment. A legacy of my pride in being honoured with an OBE and one which can be passed down the family line forever.

It would take too many words to provide a full heraldic explanation of its meaning but a potted version will provide an indication of why the delivery took fifteen months from the last of my many detailed conversations with Robert Noel, Lancaster Herald, College of Arms.

The griffin, half a lion and half an eagle comes from the generality of Wilkins. The mantle has fourteen terminal points, a reference to the bus stop where Mary and I met. The mantling of red and white are the colours of St. George and 3M. Police Support Volunteers use the livery blue and this colour is included in the ensemble. The cornucopia indicates the blessings of a safe society and growing from its foot is a white rose that Mary bore at her wedding. The honeysuckle is the flower of Warwickshire where the self-build house is situated. The snowflake is the flower of Berkshire where we now live. The points of the white ribbons represent the grandchildren. The red streamer emanating from the beacon (a symbol of vigilance and protection), is the colour of St. Stephen. The Blue, St. Christopher and the gold St. Simon (Peter). The motto comes from my belief that the family should always be proud and pleasant to everyone.

How awe inspiring to have the important things in life, many of which I have written about in this book, captured in a legacy that will remain in our family line forever.

## Personally Speaking

I have benefited from the important things in life: A devoted mother, a loving caring wife, three great children, eight smashing grandchildren, and loyal enduring friends; Peter, Marion, Keith, Alma, Graham, Elaine, Bob, Kathy, Trevor and Brenda.

Having the precious support of family and friends has allowed me to follow my dreams and take calculated risks. Providentially, most of the life changing decisions have worked out.

Is this luck? I think the words spoken by Frank Sinatra somewhat mirror my life.

"People often remark that I'm pretty lucky. Luck is only important in so far as getting the chance to sell yourself at the right moment. After that, you've got to have talent and know how to use it."

My willingness to try things though has revealed a wimpish streak when it comes to activity associated with any form of potential danger. I have only once:

- Paraglided (I thought the rope might snap).

- Been up in a balloon (I thought the basket side too low making it easy to fall out).

- Been on Space Mountain in Disney (hated the blackness, the uncertainty).

- Been driven round Brands Hatch by a Stig type driver (he was excessively fast).

- Climbed Sydney Harbour Bridge (too uncomfortable, too high).

I do not gamble, apart from a punt on the Grand National and the occasional bet on the roulette table during a cruise. I try to think things out, experience proving that ignoring instinct often resulted in a bad decision. Investing in the world's largest companies, when I had doubts about the proposal, nearly ended in disaster, Enron and World Com going bust within two months of the outlay.

I try to make considered decisions but Graham, a mate, takes it to a new level. He is a legend, forever seeking out the best deal. It is sensible to allow him to handle matters of eating out or a weekend away, as inevitably he will obtain the most beneficial offer. His thoroughness is an admirable trait I have been unable to master and it translates into his domestic life as well. He is for instance, the one person I know who would put a spirit level onto newly laid grass to make sure it is perfectly flat. Whilst this is an extreme example of Graham's perfectionist approach, my happy-go-lucky attitude often creates more work rather than less. Keith is also very structured, never failing to return objects to their original location...in his golf bag, his car, his trouser pockets. How organised. How sensible. My normal objective is to move on as soon as possible, depositing things immediately in any available place or space. It is interesting to note that although Graham and Keith have never met, they have something else in common. They are both mad car enthusiasts.